# Arctic Ocean Shipping

# The Law of the Sea



Volumes published in this Brill Research Perspectives title are listed at *brill.com/rpls*

# Arctic Ocean Shipping

*Navigation, Security and Sovereignty in the North American Arctic*

*By*

Donald R. Rothwell

BRILL

LEIDEN | BOSTON

This paperback book edition is simultaneously published as issue 1.3 (2017) of *Law of the Sea*, DOI 10.1163/24519359-12340103.

Library of Congress Control Number: 2017963512

Typeface for the Latin, Greek, and Cyrillic scripts: "Brill". See and download: brill.com/brill-typeface.

ISBN 978-90-04-36387-8 (paperback)
ISBN 978-90-04-36388-5 (e-book)


Published by Koninklijke Brill NV, Leiden, The Netherlands.
Koninklijke Brill NV incorporates the imprints Brill, Brill Hes & De Graaf, Brill Nijhoff, Brill Rodopi, Brill Sense and Hotei Publishing.


This book is printed on acid-free paper and produced in a sustainable manner.

# Contents

# Author Biography

*Donald R. Rothwell*

is Professor of International Law at the ANU College of Law, Australian National University, where he has taught since July 2006. His research has a specific focus on the law of the sea, the law of the polar regions, and the implementation of international law within Australia as reflected in 22 books, and over 200 articles, book chapters and notes in international and Australian publications. Rothwell's recent authored, co-authored or edited books include *International Law in Australia* 3rd (Thomson Reuters, 2017) edited with Crawford; *The International Law of the Sea* 2nd (Bloomsbury, 2016) with Stephens, *The Oxford Handbook of the Law of the Sea* (OUP, 2015) with Oude Elferink, Scott and Stephens (eds). Major career works include *The Polar Regions and the Development of International Law* (CUP, 1996), and *International Law: Cases and Materials with Australian Perspectives* 3rd (CUP: IN PRESS) with Kaye, Akhtarkhavari, Davis and Saunders. Rothwell is also Co-Editor of the *Australian Year Book of International Law* and Editor-in-Chief of the Brill Research Perspectives in *The Law of the Sea.* Since 2012 he has been Rapporteur of the International Law Association (ILA) Committee on 'Baselines under the International Law of the Sea'. Rothwell was previously Challis Professor of International Law and Director of the Sydney Centre for International and Global Law, University of Sydney (2004–2006), where he had taught since 1988. He has acted as a consultant or been a member of expert groups for UNEP, UNDP, IUCN, the Australian Government, and acted as advisor to the International Fund for Animal Welfare (IFAW).

# Arctic Ocean Shipping

## *Navigation, Security and Sovereignty in the North American Arctic*

*Donald R. Rothwell*
Australian National University
*Donald.Rothwell@anu.edu.au*

### Abstract

Arctic Ocean shipping is on the brink of becoming a critical legal, geopolitical and security issue as a result of the impacts of climate change and increased interest in the Arctic Ocean from States that traditionally did not operate within the region. The law of the sea through UNCLOS provides the key legal framework for the regulation of Arctic Ocean shipping, supplemented and extended by related IMO conventions and national laws and regulations. This framework has been relied upon by the two major North American Arctic States – Canada and the United States – to develop the legal regime for the Northwest Passage and the Bering Strait. There have been historic disagreements between Canada and the United States with respect to the Northwest Passage, and while not resolved they have to date been managed through legal and political responses. Other straits may become more strategically significant as a result of climate change, including Nares Strait between Canada and Greenland. EEZ and high seas Arctic Ocean navigation by foreign flagged vessels also needs to be anticipated. Multiple issues are raised with respect to maritime security and the adequacy of the existing legal regime, including how Canada and the United States will respond to interest being expressed in Arctic shipping by Asian States such as China.

* This work brings together and consolidates some of the author's prior publications on this topic including 'Canada and the United States' in Robert C. Beckman et al (eds), *Governance of Arctic Shipping: Balancing Rights and Interests of Arctic States and User States* (Brill/Nijhoff: Leiden/Boston: 2017) 217–244; 'Arctic sovereignty and its legal significance for Canada' in Leif Christian Jensen and Geir Hønneland (eds), *Handbook of the Politics of the Arctic* (Edward Elgar, Cheltenham (UK): 2015) 247–261; 'International Straits' in Donald R. Rothwell, Alex G. Oude Elferink, Karen N. Scott and Tim Stephens (eds), *The Oxford Handbook of the Law of the Sea* (Oxford University Press, Oxford: 2015) 114–133; 'International Law and Arctic Shipping' (2013) 22 *Michigan State International Law Review* 67–99; 'International Straits and Trans-Arctic Navigation' (2012) 43 *Ocean Development and International Law* 267–282.

 | DOI 10.1163/9789004363885_002

### Keywords

Arctic – UNCLOS – shipping – Canada – United States – straits – Bering Strait – Northwest Passage – security – sovereignty

## I Introduction

There is a certain ambiguity about Arctic shipping and navigation. The Arctic Ocean at present contains no major trading routes and therefore commercial shipping is significantly less than elsewhere. Nevertheless, the Arctic Ocean continues to grow in prominence. While the Arctic Ocean has been the scene of some of the more remarkable ocean voyages, it has not been the subject of very particular attention with respect to shipping in general. This is not to suggest that shipping issues are not live in the Arctic, far from it, and with the onset of the effects of climate change there has been an upsurge of interest in Arctic shipping. Whilst the Arctic is often associated with being a hostile place for shipping, Arctic voyages of discovery are inextricably woven into the history of the Arctic and are especially associated with the major scientific expeditions of the Nineteenth and Twentieth Century.[1] Nevertheless, whilst Arctic shipping has a long history, there has been a tendency to continually underestimate its significance due to the hostility of the Arctic environment and a view that the ice-covered Arctic Ocean was not suitable for traditional surface navigation. This prevailing view of the Arctic and shipping has in recent decades been challenged on two grounds. The first is that modern technology has given ships a much great capacity to be able to operate in polar oceans if they possess ice-strengthened hulls, or are accompanied by nuclear-powered icebreakers. The second is that the previously impenetrable ice barrier of the Arctic Ocean is, due to the impacts of climate change, becoming thinner as a result of hard multi-year ice giving way in some parts of the Arctic to first-year ice which is prone to break-up during the summer meaning that more open water is appearing across the Arctic.[2] As a result of these developments the

1 The history of the development of the Arctic, especially in North America, and the maritime dimension associated with Arctic expeditions and discovery is canvassed in Shelagh D. Grant, *Polar Imperative: A History of Arctic Sovereignty in North America* (Douglas & McIntyre, Vancouver: 2011).

2 These developments are generally outlined in Lawson W. Brigham, 'The Changing Maritime Arctic and New Maritime Operations' in Robert C. Beckman et al (eds), *Governance of Arctic*

legal regime of Arctic navigation and the regulation of shipping is becoming more important which in turn places the spotlight on the law of the sea in the Arctic.

The emergence of the modern law of the sea post World War II coincided with a global economic boom as new markets emerged and trade opportunities arose. In this setting, the law of the sea had an important role to play through the ongoing realisation of the Grotian vision of the freedom of the seas, albeit one that increasingly was set within the context of more highly regulated ocean space through the four 1958 Geneva Conventions on the Law of the Sea,[3] and subsequently the 1982 United Nations Convention on the Law of the Sea (UNCLOS).[4] Even allowing for the impact of new maritime zones,[5] and the expansion in the width of the territorial sea,[6] one of the law of the sea constants has been the recognition of certain navigation rights for international shipping within the territorial sea and other maritime zones. The importance of these rights was acknowledged by the International Court of Justice in the 1949 *Corfu Channel* case,[7] when the court was prepared to accept the special status of straits used for international navigation.[8] The need for a distinctive law of the sea regime dealing with straits arose because of the significance of international straits, or 'international maritime highways', to commerce. International maritime trade had historically developed using the shortest navigable route between ports and reliance was placed upon straits connecting one high seas area with another as a means of safe and expeditious passage. In

*Shipping* (Brill/Nijhoff, Leiden/Boston: 2017) 3–23; and Peter Wadhams, *A Farewell to Ice* (Allen Lane, London: 2016).

3 The term 'Geneva Conventions on the Law of the Sea' include the four conventions concluded at the 1958 Geneva conference: 1958 Convention on the Territorial Sea and Contiguous Zone, 516 *UNTS* 206; 1958 Convention on the High Sea, 450 *UNTS* 82; 1958 Convention on Fishing and Conservation of the Living Resources of the High Seas, 559 *UNTS* 286; 1958 Convention on the Continental Shelf, 499 *UNTS* 312.

4 1982 United Nations Convention on the Law of the Sea, 1833 *UNTS* 397 (hereafter UNCLOS).

5 Such as the exclusive economic zone, provided for in Part V, UNCLOS.

6 Article 3, UNCLOS.

7 *Corfu Channel case* (United Kingdom v Albania) [1949] ICJ Reps p. 4.

8 See discussion on the ongoing significance of this decision of the International Court of Justice in Karine Bannelier, Theodore Christakis, and Sarah Heathcote (eds), *The ICJ and the Evolution of International Law: The enduring impact of the Corfu Channel case* (Routledge, New York: 2012).

Europe, the Straits of Gibraltar,[9] Straits of Dover,[10] the Danish Straits, and the Turkish Straits[11] all acquired considerable strategic, political and commercial significance because of the volume of maritime traffic supplying international trade that passed through those waters.[12] Beyond Europe, other straits had similar strategic, political and commercial importance, including the Straits of Malacca and Singapore,[13] Sunda Strait, Tawian (Formosa) Strait, Torres Strait,[14] Bass Strait,[15] Juan de Fuca Strait, Florida Strait, and the Straits of Magellan.[16] Through first the regime of innocent passage,[17] and then the transit passage regime,[18] the law of the sea sought to accommodate the special circumstances of straits and their pivotal role as part of a maritime highway that connected adjoining oceans and high seas areas. Indeed, a trade off that took place during the Third United Nations Conference on the Law of the Sea was counterbalancing the rights and interests of coastal states with the equivalent rights and interests of maritime states. Part III of the UNCLOS and the regime of straits used for international navigation very much reflected a pivotal compromise within the new law of the sea and has proven to be central to the maintenance and development of international trade through straits around the world.

The development of international maritime trade in the second half of the Twentieth Century, and the accompanying law, was inevitably focussed on the major trading routes and the straits and oceans that supported that trade. The effect of the prominence of the Atlantic and Pacific Oceans and their adjoining seas and straits was that some of the world's oceans were largely ignored in a navigational sense. In that respect, the polar oceans more generally have not been the subject of significant maritime interest and this is primarily because they have proven to be particularly inaccessible due to wide spread ice cover making any form of surface navigation often impossible. An additional

9 Scott C. Truver, *The Strait of Gibraltar and the Mediterranean* (Sijthoff & Noordhoff, Alphen Aan Den Rijn: 1980).

10 Luc Cuyvers, *The Strait of Dover* (Martinus Nijhoff, Dordrecht: 1986).

11 Ünlü Nihan, *The legal regime of the Turkish Straits* (Martinus Nijhoff, The Hague: 2002).

12 Erik Brüel, *International Straits* Vol II (Sweet & Maxwell, London: 1947).

13 Michael Leifer, *International Straits of the World: Malacca, Singapore and Indonesia* (Sijthoff & Noordhoff, Alphen Aan Den Rijn: 1978).

14 Stuart B. Kaye, *The Torres Strait* (Martinus Nijhoff, Boston: 1997).

15 Donald R. Rothwell, 'International Straits and UNCLOS: An Australian Case Study' (1992) 23 *Journal of Maritime Law and Commerce* 461–483.

16 Michael A. Morris, *The Strait of Magellan* (Martinus Nijhoff, Dordrecht: 1989).

17 Articles 14–23, Convention on the Territorial Sea and Contiguous Zone; Articles 17–32, UNCLOS.

18 Articles 37–44, UNCLOS.

factor has been their remote location from markets. Accordingly, there has been little economic incentive for major shipping lines to develop polar trade routes. An exception has been the Northeast Passage and the Northern Sea Route. Both predominantly fall within the reach of Russia's maritime zones, and as Russia has sought to develop its Arctic/Siberian coastline there has been longstanding interest in the viability of these trade routes and also their associated legal regime.[19] The other exception has been the Northwest Passage, the status of which has been the subject of disagreement between Canada and the United States.[20] A navigable Northwest Passage permits trade routes through the Canadian Arctic Archipelago between Alaska and the East Coast of the United States, and if access via the Bering Strait is also considered then trade routes from east Asia also become viable. Over the past decade the Northwest Passage has also taken on additional significance due to the growing number of cruise ships that seek to transit the Passage, or at least gain access to some parts from either the eastern or western approaches. Climate change has also had a profound impact upon how the law of the sea is seen as being applicable in the Arctic. Not only has it refocussed interest on the Northeast and Northwest Passages, but it has also contributed to increased debate over the importance of maritime zones such as continental shelf claims that extend not only within 200 nautical miles of the Arctic coastline, but also potentially and consistent with the provisions of Article 76 of the UNCLOS into the central Arctic Ocean.[21]

---

19 See R.D. Brubaker, *The Russian Arctic Straits* (Martinus Nijhoff, Leiden: 2005); Leonid Timchenko, 'The Northern Sea Route: Russian Management and Jurisdiction over Navigation in Arctic Seas', in Alex G. Oude Elferink and Donald R. Rothwell (eds), *The Law of the Sea and Polar Maritime Delimitation and Jurisdiction* (Martinus Nijhoff, The Hague: 2001) 269–291; Willy Ostreng, 'The Northern Sea Route: a new era in Soviet policy?' (1991) 22 *Ocean Development and International Law* 259–287.

20 There is extensive literature on this issue; see e.g. Ted L. McDorman, *Salt Water Neighbors*, (Oxford University Press, New York: 2009) 225–254; Michael Byers and Suzanne Lalonde, 'Who controls the Northwest Passage?' (2009) 42 *Vanderbilt Journal of Transnational Law* 1133–1210; Donald R. Rothwell, 'The Canadian – U.S. Northwest Passage Dispute: A Reassessment' (1993) 26 *Cornell International Law Journal* 331–372; Donat Pharand, *The Northwest Passage Arctic Straits* (Martinus Nijhoff, Dordrecht: 1984).

21 See e.g. Timo Koivurova, 'The Actions of Arctic States Respecting the Continental Shelf: A Reflective Essay' (2011) 42 *Ocean Development and International Law* 211–226; Vladimir Jares, 'The Continental Shelf Beyond 200 Nautical Miles: The Work of the Commission on the Limits of the Continental Shelf and the Arctic' (2009) 42 *Vanderbilt Journal of Transnational Law* 1265–1306; Mel Weber, 'Defining the outer limits of the continental shelf across the Arctic basin: the Russian submission, states' rights, boundary delimitation

The combination of climate change and the potential for at least a partially ice free Arctic Ocean,[22] combined with an acknowledgement of continental shelf rights in an area that is increasingly becoming more accessible to a range of maritime activities has generated considerable political interest, with accompanying legal and policy implications.[23] One particular dimension of this renewed Arctic interest has been the attention given to Arctic shipping in general, and navigational issues in particular.[24] The 2009 *Arctic Maritime Shipping Assessment (AMSA) Report* highlighted this increased level of interest.[25] The AMSA *Report* indicated that during the 2004 survey year there were nearly 6,000 individual vessels operating in the Arctic region, many making multiple voyages. It was observed that "[n]early all shipping in the Arctic today is destinational, conducted for community re-supply, marine tourism and moving natural resources out of the Arctic."[26] However what was also apparent from the *AMSA Report* was the potential for an increase in not only destinational Arctic shipping, but also trans-Arctic shipping, that is shipping that crosses the Arctic Ocean from a point of entry to a point of exit. Trans-Arctic shipping routes may operate via the Northeast or Northwest Passages, in which case the Bering Strait becomes pivotal as a point of access or egress.[27] There is also the potential for shipping routes across the central Arctic Ocean from the

---

and Arctic regional cooperation' (2009) 24 *International Journal of Marine and Coastal Law* 653–681.

22 The first time that consistent reports emerged of the Northwest Passage being ice free was 2007, which coincided with a then record minimum sea ice extent being recorded for Arctic sea ice: John Roach, "Arctic Melt Opens Northwest Passage," National Geographic News, September 17, 2007, at: https://news.nationalgeographic.com/news/2007/09/070917-northwest-passage.html (last accessed on 1 November 2017); and John Roach, "Arctic Ice at All-Time Low," National Geographic News, August 20, 2007, at: https://news.nationalgeographic.com/news/2007/08/070820-global-warming.html (last accessed on 1 November 2017).

23 See e.g. James Kraska (ed), *Arctic Security in a Age of Climate Change* (Cambridge University Press, Cambridge: 2011); Scott G. Borgerson, 'Arctic Meltdown: The Economic and Security Implications of Global Warming' (2008) 87 *Foreign Affairs* 63–77.

24 See e.g. Aldo Chircop, 'The Growth of International Shipping in the Arctic: Is a Regulatory Review Timely?' (2009) 24 *International Journal of Marine and Coastal Law* 355–380; E.J. Molenaar, 'Arctic Marine Shipping: Overview of the International Legal Framework, Gaps, and Options' (2009) 18 *Journal of Transnational Law and Policy* 289–325.

25 Arctic Council, *Arctic Marine Shipping Assessment 2009 Report* (Arctic Council, Tromsø: 2009) (AMSA Report).

26 Ibid., at pp. 4–5.

27 See Molenaar (n. 24), at pp. 292–293.

Pacific via Bering Strait through to the Atlantic by way of the Denmark or Fram Straits. Each of these routes would considerably reduce the distance travelled on existing trade routes. For example, a trans-Arctic shipping route through the Bering Strait, across the Arctic Ocean and then via the Fram and Greenland Straits to Iceland is almost 5,000 nautical miles shorter than using the Panama Canal between Hamburg and Yokohama.[28] Polar class vessels, capable of operating in a substantially ice-reduced Arctic are being built in order to take advantage of these opportunities.[29] China, a non-Arctic State but with growing interests in the Arctic, is currently building its second Arctic ice-breaker and has also indicated an interest in developing nuclear ice-breakers.[30] One of the implications arising from these developments is that the straits that provide access to the Arctic Ocean from both the Atlantic and Pacific Oceans will become more commercially and strategically significant and the legal regime that operates within those straits will likewise be important.

The effect of these developments has been to give greater attention to shipping throughout the Arctic, the potential for Arctic shipping to continue to grow especially as the Arctic Ocean becomes more ice free, and ultimately the legal regime for the regulation of Arctic shipping.[31] While historically the Northwest Passage has since the 1970s been the focal point of analysis with respect to Arctic navigational rights and freedoms vis-à-vis Canada and the United States in the North American Arctic,[32] the Bering Strait is also beginning to gain attention.[33] The importance of the Bering Strait to Arctic navigation was highlighted by the *AMSA Report*.[34] For the first time, an effort was made to comprehensively assess the status of Arctic shipping. Particular attention was given to Arctic navigational routes and not only the Northwest Passage and Northeast Passage (Northern Sea Route),[35] but also the Bering

28 Chircop (n. 24) at p. 356; see also Borgerson (n. 23) at p. 70.

29 Chircop (n. 24) at p. 357.

30 Atle Staalesen, 'China is building its second icebreaker domestically' *Arctic Now* (28 September 2017) at: https://www.arcticnow.com/business/shipping/2017/09/28/china-is-building-its-second-icebreaker-domestically/ (last accessed on 1 November 2017).

31 See generally Tessa Mendez, 'Thin Ice, Shifting Geopolitics: The Legal Implications of Arctic Ice Melt' (2010) 38 *Denver Journal of International Law and Policy* 527–547.

32 See e.g. Donat Pharand, 'The Arctic Waters and the Northwest Passage: A Final Revisit', (2007) 38 *Ocean Development and International Law* 3–60; Rothwell (n. 20).

33 See e.g. Andrew Hartsig et al, 'Arctic Bottleneck: Protecting the Bering Strait from Increased Vessel Traffic', (2012) 10 *Ocean and Coastal Law Journal* 35–87.

34 *AMSA Report* (n. 25) at pp. 106–109.

35 Ibid. at pp. 112–119.

Strait and regional future scenarios.[36] In this respect not only did the *AMSA Report* highlight the navigational and strategic importance of the Bering Strait, but also the role of the US in its ongoing regulation and management.

The *AMSA Report* and the ongoing increase in Arctic ship movements have also focused attention on Arctic Ocean 'chokepoints', that is, those straits and associated waterways, which allow for access to and from the Arctic Ocean.[37] While certain bodies of water provide access to the Arctic, consideration also needs to be given to the 'exit' points. In this respect, Honderich has observed:

> What points there are, are guarded and narrow. Exit from the Arctic can be made from only four points: out the Bering Sea, which is treacherously shallow; out through the thin gap between Greenland and Canada; out through the maze of the Canadian archipelago and the Northwest Passage; and finally out the widest route, the Greenland-Iceland-United Kingdom (GIUK) Gap, which is carefully monitored by NATO.[38]

The Bering Strait and Fram Strait are of particular significance because they allow for access to and between the Pacific and Atlantic Oceans via the Arctic Ocean,[39] diminishing reliance upon routing via the Suez and Panama Canals. In this respect, the Arctic Ocean is distinctive from the world's other oceans in that it is the only ocean surrounded by continents, and where there is only one major high seas point of access to the Atlantic Ocean through the Greenland and Norwegian Seas.[40]

The Bering Strait is perhaps the most strategically located of the current Arctic 'chokepoints' given its location at the northern limit of the Pacific Ocean, and the direct access that it provides between the Bering Sea and Chukchi Sea into the Arctic Ocean. Given the rise in Arctic shipping, especially along the

---

36 Ibid. at pp. 106–109.

37 Note the *AMSA Report* specifically refers to the Bering Strait as a 'crucial chokepoint'; Ibid. at p. 129; see also p. 109.

38 John Honderich, *Arctic Imperative: Is Canada Losing the North?* (University of Toronto Press, Toronto: 1987) 93–94. For further assessment of the GIUK Gap and its strategic significance, especially during the Cold War, see Hugh Faringdon, *Strategic Geography: NATO, the Warsaw Pact, and the Superpowers* 2nd (Routledge, London: 1989) 175–179.

39 *AMSA Report* (n. 25) at p. 18.

40 The Greenland Sea is that body of water to the north of Iceland and lies between Greenland and Svalbard and via Fram Strait provides access to the Arctic Ocean; the Norwegian Sea is that body of water off the coast of Norway which between Svalbard and Norway provides access to the Barents Sea and the Northern Sea Route.

Northern Sea Route, the Bering Strait's significance to Arctic navigation will only continue to increase in the future especially due to its proximity to major trading powers, such as China, Japan and South Korea.[41] The Bering Strait will also be important if the Northwest Passage becomes a major Arctic navigation route because of the access that it provides to the Beaufort Sea for ships that are navigating west to east along the Northwest Passage en route to the US East Coast and the Atlantic Ocean. The presence of six commercial ports within the Bering Strait region – three American and three Russian – located to the south of the Strait further emphasises the current and future commercial capability for shipping through the region.[42] The Bering Strait is also recognised by the US Department of Defense for its strategic importance, with a May 2011 Departmental publication acknowledging that:

> An increase in maritime traffic between Asia and Europe, or Russia, could also raise the prominence of the Bering Strait as a strategic chokepoint and heighten the geostrategic importance of the Arctic region.[43]

Canada and the United States, two of the larger and politically powerful Arctic States, have had a longstanding interest in Arctic shipping and navigation. For Canada, shipping and navigation were not only critical for the initial exploration and discovery of the Canadian North, but were also pivotal to the development of the region. The Northwest Passage, an iconic Arctic waterway which is deeply ingrained in the Canadian psyche,[44] has also proven to be contentious

---

41 United States Coast Guard, *Arctic Strategy* (United States Coast Guard, Washington: 2013) 5, cites a 118 per cent increase in maritime transit through the Bering Strait from 2008–2012.

42 *AMSA Report* (n. 25) at p. 108; these being the US ports of Nome, Kotzebue and the DeLong Mountain Transportation System port that serves Red Dog Mine; and the Russian ports of Provideniya, Anadyr and Egvekinot.

43 Department of Defense (USA), *Report to Congress on Arctic Operations and the Northwest Passage* (Department of Defense, Washington: May 2011) 9; see also United States Coast Guard (n. 41) at p. 13.

44 Mieke Coppes and Victoria Herrmann, *First Past the Pole: Harper, Trudeau, and Canada's Arctic Values* (The Arctic Institute, Centre for Circumpolar Security Studies, Washington: October 30, 2015) at http://www.thearcticinstitute.org/2015/10/first-past-the-pole.html (last accessed on 1 November 2017); see generally Lee-Anne Broadhead, 'Canadian sovereignty verses northern security: the case for updating our mental map of the Arctic' in Leif Christian Jensen and Geir Hønneland (eds), *Handbook of the Politics of the Arctic* (Edward Elgar, Cheltenham, UK: 2015) 281–297.

in Canadian-United States relations given differing views as to its status. For the United States, shipping and navigation has likewise been critical to the development of Alaska both economically and strategically, while US strategic interests across the Arctic as a whole have also relied heavily upon the freedom of navigation. When these historical factors are combined with the impacts of climate change and a partially ice free Arctic Ocean,[45] which in turn is attracting significant interest from states that traditionally have not had an interest in Arctic affairs, a range of diplomatic, legal and policy implications are confronting Arctic shipping and navigation.

This focus in recent years upon Arctic shipping has also come at a time when Arctic governance has been the subject of much recent analysis as the Arctic Council has become more proactive in dealing with a range of Arctic issues and beginning to facilitate new Arctic agreements. During this period there has also been ongoing debate as to the adequacy of Arctic governance arrangements, including whether there is the need for an 'Arctic Treaty'.[46] While these debates ultimately have not gained much traction, partly due to the development of the Arctic Council, they reflected a sense that the Arctic was becoming a region of greater global significance. In that sense, the Arctic has become 'globalised' as an issue area thereby raising issues associated with its governance and legal framework.[47]

This monograph seeks to explore these issues by focussing on the North American Arctic which encompasses the waters from the Bering Strait east to the Atlantic over which Canada and the United States have particular interests.

---

45 See 2017 assessments in 'Summer Sea Ice Melt in the Arctic' *Science Daily* (July 24, 2017) at: https://www.sciencedaily.com/releases/2017/07/170724133153.htm (last accessed on 1 November 2017); 'Arctic Sea Ice Again Shows Considerable Melting' *Science Daily* (September 15, 2017) at: https://www.sciencedaily.com/releases/2017/09/170915103604.htm (last accessed on 1 November 2017).

46 See the discussion in Hans H. Hertell, 'Arctic melt: the tipping point for an Arctic Treaty' (2009) 21 *Georgetown International Environmental Law Review* 565–589; Molly Watson, 'An Arctic treaty: a solution to the international dispute over the polar region' (2009) 14 *Ocean and Coastal Law Journal* 307–334; Donald R. Rothwell, 'The Arctic in International Affairs: Time for a New Regime?' (2008) XV (1) *Brown Journal of World Affairs* 241–253.

47 This is reflected in the surge in Arctic and polar related geopolitical discourse in works such as Leif Christian Jensen and Geir Hønneland (eds), *Handbook of the Politics of the Arctic* (Edward Elgar, Cheltenham, UK: 2015); Richard C. Powell and Klaus Dodds (eds), *Polar Geopolitics?* (Edward Elgar, Cheltenham, UK: 2014); Oran R. Young, Jong Deog Kim and Yoon Hyung Kim (eds), *The Arctic in World Affairs* (Korea Maritime Institute/East-West Centre, Seoul/Honolulu: 2013).

Waters on the margins such as those between Canada and Denmark (with respect to Greenland) and the north western Atlantic are also assessed due to the context they provide for better appreciating Canadian and United States Arctic interests. The Russian and Scandinavian Arctic are not considered in any detail, other than to provide context and background. It is acknowledged that there is a significant body of literature and scholarship associated with Russian Arctic shipping, particularly regarding the Northeast Passage/Northern Sea Route, however the constraints upon this current study preclude assessment of those issues at this time.

The study commences first with an assessment of the legal regime of the Arctic in general terms, and then specifically in the context of the law of the sea and related aspects of maritime law. Consideration is given to Arctic governance, and developments over the past decade that are relevant to an understanding of the Arctic legal regime. The work then moves to an assessment of the distinctive navigation and shipping issues that exist in the North American Arctic and related waters. Particular attention is given to Canada's position with respect to the Northwest Passage and the US position with respect to the Bering Strait. Other important Arctic waterways within the broader North American Arctic are also considered, including the issues associated with navigation through the Exclusive Economic Zone (EEZ). Maritime security in the Arctic will also be generally considered as it provides an additional context to appreciating issues confronting Canada and the US in the Arctic. The monograph ends with some conclusions and reflections.

## II Arctic Ocean Legal Regime

To begin it is necessary to assess and reflect upon the extent of the legal regime that applies in the Arctic, whether that be the application of general international law, specific bodies of international law such as that found in the law of the sea, or in regional or national laws that specifically apply within the Arctic. This initial review will provide a basis upon which to then assess how international law, and particularly the law of the sea, has been applied and interpreted in the North American Arctic.

### A *International Law in the Arctic Ocean*

The Arctic as a region is not exempt from the application of general international law, whether it be customary international law or treaty. In that respect, international law applies in the Arctic in the same manner as it does elsewhere around the world, including in the other polar region, Antarctica.[48] Nevertheless, there has been something of a view that some elements of international law could not apply in the Arctic because the region was generally inaccessible and the Arctic Ocean in particular, was ice-covered, thereby making it distinctive from the world's other oceans to which the law of the sea generally applied. A further contrast was also drawn between the Arctic and Antarctica in that the southern polar region was the subject of its own distinctive regional treaty which had provided the foundation for the development of what has become known as the Antarctic Treaty System, which provides a distinctive regional legal regime for Antarctica whilst also interacting with the global international legal regime.[49]

However as the Arctic has become more accessible, there has been an acceptance that international law has just as much a role in the region as it does elsewhere with the law of the sea in particular assuming significance given how the Arctic Ocean dominates the region. In this respect, it needs to be recalled that the international law of the sea has been through a process of ongoing development since the Seventeenth Century and over the past 60 years has been codified in the four Geneva Conventions of 1958, and then in UNCLOS which entered into force in 1994. UNCLOS unquestionably creates a legal foundation for the regulation and management of the Arctic Ocean and its associated and adjacent waters,[50] including the national maritime zones and internal waters of Arctic coastal States. With the exception of the United States, all of the Arctic littoral states are parties to UNCLOS, and the US position is that it considers UNCLOS to substantially reflect customary international law such that it adheres to its principal provisions.[51]

---

48 The author's discussion of this issue can be found in more detail in Donald R. Rothwell, *The Polar Regions and the Development of International Law* (Cambridge University Press, Cambridge: 1996).

49 See generally Davor Vidas (ed), *Protecting the Polar Marine Environment: Law and Policy for Pollution Prevention* (Cambridge University Press, Cambridge: 2000).

50 Louise Angelique de La Fayette, 'Oceans Governance in the Arctic' (2008) 23 *International Journal of Marine and Coastal Law* 531–566 who at p. 532 observed: 'The ... (UNCLOS) has established the international legal regime governing the division of ocean space, sovereign rights over ocean resources, protection of the marine environment and the conduct of activities in and under the Arctic Ocean.'

51 J. Ashley Roach and Robert W. Smith, *Excessive Maritime Claims* 3rd (Martinus Nijhoff, Leiden/Boston: 2012) have observed at p. 639 that: "*The Commander's Handbook on the Law of Naval Operations* was developed to provide definitive guidance to US operating forces.... It states that the [UNCLOS] codifies existing and emerging customary

The significance of the law of the sea for the Arctic is further reaffirmed by the May 2008 Ilulissat Declaration,[52] which was issued by the five Arctic littoral states with interests over the Arctic Ocean: Canada, Denmark (Greenland), Norway, Russian Federation, and USA.[53] The Declaration is prefaced by acknowledging that the Arctic Ocean is at the threshold of significant change. Reference is made to climate change, melting of the ice, potential impacts upon vulnerable ecosystems, the livelihoods of local inhabitants and indigenous communities, and potential exploitation of natural resources. The littoral Arctic States note that by virtue of their sovereignty, sovereign rights and jurisdiction in large areas of the Arctic Ocean they are "in a unique position to address these possibilities and challenges". The Declaration observes that "an extensive international legal framework applies to the Arctic Ocean", however no precise reference is made to any particular international instrument such as the UNCLOS. Nevertheless, the Declaration is very precise as to what it then has to say about the law of the sea, which is as follows:

> ... the law of the sea provides for important rights and obligations concerning the delineation of the outer limits of the continental shelf, the protection of the marine environment, including ice-covered areas, freedom of navigation, marine scientific research, and other uses of the sea. We remain committed to this legal framework and to the orderly settlement of any possible overlapping claims.

Observing that "[t]his framework provides a solid foundation for responsible management by the five coastal States and other users of this Ocean through national implementation and application of relevant provisions", the Declaration proceeds to conclusively state that "We therefore see no need to develop a new comprehensive international legal regime to govern the Arctic Ocean." The Declaration goes on to identify the need for measures to protect and preserve the Arctic Ocean marine environment, safety of life at sea, and closer cooperation on these and related Arctic Ocean issues.

---

international law pertaining to navigation and overflight and, as such, is binding upon all U.S., forces operating in the maritime environment."

52 (2009) 48 ILM 382 (Ilulissat Declaration).

53 While Finland, Iceland, and Norway are also founding members of the Arctic Council and as such comprise the 'Arctic Eight' alongside Canada, Denmark, Norway, the Russian Federation and the USA, none of these three states have coastlines washed by the Arctic Ocean proper, nor do they assert maritime claims into the central Arctic Ocean.

Other than the law of the sea, the Arctic is also subject to a host of other general and specific international law and those that particularly deal with shipping are noted in more detail below. As such, the relevant international law dealing with sovereign title over territory applies to the terrestrial areas of the Arctic and indeed was pivotal in resolving disputes between Denmark and Norway over the status of Greenland.[54] Likewise, international human rights law also applies in the Arctic,[55] as does international environmental law including the 1946 International Convention for the Regulation of Whaling which has specific relevance for many of the Arctic states.[56] In summary then, the Arctic is subject to the same body of international law as that which applies globally though given the nature of the region the law of the sea has more particular relevance than may be the case elsewhere.

### B *Arctic Sovereignty and International Law*

State sovereignty and the effective assertion of territorial title to polar areas has held a fascination for international lawyers for over a century. This has no doubt been driven by the relative contemporary exploration of polar areas, which resulted in both the North and South Pole being first reached early in the Twentieth Century, and also because of the challenges in effectively asserting sovereignty over polar areas. As a result, notwithstanding discovery of polar areas and the assertions of title that were often associated with those discoveries, claims over Antarctica or the Arctic represented classic examples of inchoate titles in need of perfection. That the *Eastern Greenland* case acknowledged the challenges associated with the effective assertion of title over polar areas,[57] provided an additional legal basis for appreciating the distinctiveness of these issues.

Throughout the Twentieth Century the effective exercise of sovereignty over polar areas was problematic given their relative inaccessibility and distance from metropolitan lands. Judge Huber in *Island of Palmas* recognised that differential standards may apply "according to conditions of time and place",

---

54 See *Legal Status of Eastern Greenland* (Denmark v Norway) [1933] PCIJ Rep (Ser. A/B) No. 53.

55 There is an extensive literature with respect to the specific human rights issues confronting the Inuit in the Arctic, see generally Gudmundur Alfredsson, 'Arctic governance: Human Rights, Good Governance and Democracy' (2012) 4 *The Yearbook of Polar Law* 141–153.

56 161 *UNTS* 74.

57 *Legal Status of Eastern Greenland* (Denmark v Norway) [1933] PCIJ Rep (Ser. A/B) No. 53.

and also whether territory was inhabited or uninhabited.[58] However, it was in *Eastern Greenland* that the Permanent Court of International Justice (PCIJ) made express reference to the particular challenges associated with fulfilling the requirements of effective occupation in the polar regions, noting that:

> It is impossible to read the records of the decisions in cases as to territorial sovereignty without observing that in many cases the tribunal has been satisfied with very little in the way of the actual exercise of sovereign rights, provided that the other State could not make out a superior claim. This is particularly true in the case of claims to sovereignty over areas in thinly populated or unsettled countries.[59]

While publicists have agreed that the strict standards applied to more temperate lands do not apply to the polar regions,[60] they have maintained that some of the traditional incidents of effective occupation must still be made out. This opens for consideration whether different standards should be applied to the determination of polar territorial claims in the Twenty-First Century than was previously the case. Two factors immediately would appear relevant. The first is that the polar regions are now more accessible than was the case at the time they were first discovered and when the early cases were decided. While they cannot necessarily be equated with 'temperate lands', they can be reached with an ease that would have been unimaginable a century ago and as such no longer are as 'distant' as previously imagined. The second is that modern technology has rendered the polar regions capable of settlement in much the same fashion as other parts of the globe. In the Arctic, the Russian city of Murmansk is the biggest city north of the Arctic Circle with a population of over 300,000.[61] While Canada's Arctic population is much smaller than that of the Russian

58 *The Netherlands v United States of America* (1928) 2 Reports of International Arbitral Awards 829, 840.

59 *Legal Status of Eastern Greenland* (Denmark v Norway) [1933] PCIJ Rep (Ser. A/B) No. 53, 46.

60 See F.M. Auburn, *Antarctic Law and Politics* (C.Hurst, London: 1982) 13; Gillian D. Triggs, *International Law and Australian Sovereignty in Antarctica* (Legal Books, Sydney: 1986) 82; Philip C. Jessup and Howard J. Taubenfeld, *Controls for Outer Space and the Antarctic Analogy* (Columbia University Press, New York: 1959) 141.

61 Charles Emmerson, *The Future History of the Arctic* (Public Affairs, London: 2010) 68; while 2017 statistics suggest that the population of Murmansk has declined it is reported that the population of the Kola Peninsula is 1.12 million: Thomas Nilsen, 'Murmansk and Arkhangelsk population continues to decline' *The Independent Barents Observer* (September 28, 2017) at: https://thebarentsobserver.com/en/life-and-public/2017/09/

Federation, over 100,000 Canadians live north of the Arctic Circle which is approximately ten percent of the total population beyond the Arctic Circle and is slowly increasing.[62]

An unresolved aspect of polar sovereignty is the status of claims based upon the so-called 'sector theory' which is that states can assert a territorial claim along lines of latitude that run directly to the Pole, thereby effectively dividing up the region. A significant feature of Antarctic claims, for example, is that with the exception of Norway they are all framed around a sector as all the claims commence at points along the Antarctic coast and converge along degrees of longitude at the geographic South Pole. The sector theory has also been influential in debates over Arctic territorial claims, where it was thought to have been based upon principles such as contiguity, 'hinterland' or the 'spheres of influence' doctrine.[63] In the Arctic, sector claims are based on the geographic proximity of the claimant state, and have from time to time been asserted as a basis of claim to Arctic lands by Canada and Russia. Ultimately, sector theory has never been the subject of final determination by an international court or tribunal, has never been officially relied upon by claimant states to polar areas, and has been subject to widespread critique from commentators. Crawford has assessed the principle as one that "remains a rough method of delimitation, and has not become a separate rule of law,"[64] while Shaw characterises it as a "political proposition".[65] Crawford's further reservations extend to the observation that the sector principle inherits some of the defects of contiguity, that "its application is a little absurd insofar as there is a claim to a narrow sliver of sovereignty stretching to the Pole", and that it cannot apply to areas of the high seas.[66] It can therefore be observed that while the standard international law principles associated with the assertion of sovereignty and the

---

murmansk-and-arkhangelsk-population-continues-decline (last accessed on 1 November 2017).

62 Levon Sevunts, 'Census 2016: Nunavut leads Canada's population growth' *Eye on the Arctic* (8 February 2017) at: http://www.rcinet.ca/eye-on-the-arctic/2017/02/08/census-2016-nunavut-leads-canadas-population-growth/ (last accessed on 1 November 2017).

63 See Robert Jennings and Arthur Watts, *Oppenheim's International Law* Vol 1, Pts 2–4 (Longman, Harlow, UK: 1992) 693; Gustav Smedal, *Acquisition of Sovereignty over Polar Areas* (I Kommisjon Hos Jacob Dybwad, Oslo: 1931) 54–76; Oscar Svarlien, 'The Sector Principle in Law and Practice' (1960) 10 *Polar Record* 248–263.

64 James Crawford, *Brownlie's Principles of Public International Law* 8th (Oxford University Press, Oxford: 2012) 241; Auburn (n. 60) at p. 31.

65 Malcolm N. Shaw, *International Law* 6th (Cambridge University Press, Cambridge: 2008) 535.

66 Crawford (n. 64) at p. 241.

perfection of territorial title apply to polar areas, there has also been some recognition of the distinctive aspects of polar sovereignty. Whether those points of distinction, including particular theories that have been applied in the past to polar areas such as the sector theory, have much contemporary application is a matter for determination.

### C *Arctic Shipping and International Law*

The growth in Arctic shipping as outlined in the *AMSA Report* has increasingly shone the spotlight onto the legal regulatory framework for Arctic shipping. During the late Twentieth Century the attention that was given to this issue was nearly exclusively focussed on the particular legal regimes that governed navigation through the Northwest Passage, and specifically the differing views of Canada and the United States over what legal regime applied within those waters,[67] and on the other hand the legal regulation by the USSR and Russian Federation of shipping through the Northern Sea Route.[68] While the specific legal navigational regimes through those waters remain significant, recently increased attention has been given to broader issues associated with the legal regulation of Arctic shipping in the increasingly open waters of the Arctic Ocean,[69] of which the *AMSA Report* has been the most significant.

In this respect it has been observed above that the UNCLOS creates the core legal framework for all activities associated with the Arctic maritime domain, and this certainly extends to include shipping. There are two central components to how the UNCLOS impacts upon the Arctic in this respect. The first is that the UNCLOS provides the basis for the assertion of the complete range of contemporary maritime zones commencing with the territorial sea (12 nautical miles),[70] contiguous zone (24 nautical miles),[71] exclusive economic zone (EEZ) (200 nautical miles),[72] and the continental shelf (200 nautical miles minimum with capacity for expansion to approximately 350 nautical miles).[73] Conterminous with the continental shelf beyond 200 nautical miles are the

67 See e.g. Donat Pharand, 'The Northwest Passage in International Law' (1979) 17 *Canadian Yearbook of International Law* 99–133; Ted.L. McDorman, 'In the Wake of the Polar Sea: Canadian Jurisdiction and the Northwest Passage' (1986) 10 *Marine Policy* 243–257.

68 See e.g. Brubaker (n. 19); see on both of these issues Erik Franckx, *Maritime Claims in the Arctic: Canadian and Russian Perspectives* (Martinus Nijhoff, Dordrecht/Boston/London: 1993).

69 See e.g. Chircop (n. 24); Molenaar (n. 24).

70 Article 3, UNCLOS.

71 Article 33, UNCLOS.

72 Article 57, UNCLOS.

73 Article 76, UNCLOS.

high seas, which also exists beyond the limits of the EEZ.[74] These various maritime zones give to Arctic coastal states sovereignty over their adjacent territorial sea, and beyond that sovereign rights mixed with specific jurisdiction over for example the protection and management of the marine environment.[75] The other significant dimension of the UNCLOS is that it provides for the recognition of navigational rights and freedoms for foreign shipping and this is particularly significant in the context of the right of innocent passage through the territorial sea,[76] the right of transit passage through international straits,[77] and the rights of high seas freedom of navigation over those areas of EEZ and continental shelf claimed by a coastal state subject to specific constraints that apply within those maritime areas.[78] The consequence of these dual sets of measures under the UNCLOS is that Arctic littoral states have been able to claim a range of maritime zones under which they have been able to enjoy certain rights and privileges, while at the same time the international community and other Arctic states have an assurance that navigational rights and freedoms can continue to be exercised throughout the Arctic, or that in some instances these rights can actually be enjoyed for the very first time as a result of the effects of climate change and the opening of the region to greater shipping opportunities.

The UNCLOS is not, however, a comprehensive legal framework for all shipping operations and is significantly supplemented by a separate body of international law dealing with ship-sourced marine pollution and another body of international maritime law that regulates a variety of aspects of shipping operations. The 1973 International Convention for the Prevention of Pollution from Ships (MARPOL),[79] as amended by its 1978 Protocol, provides the core legal

74 Article 86, UNCLOS which is the first article found in Part VII of the UNCLOS and which provides: "The provisions of this Part apply to all parts of the sea that are not included in the exclusive economic zone, in the territorial sea or in the internal waters of a State". However, Article 58 notes that the freedoms of navigation and overflight referred to in Article 87 with respect to the high seas also apply within the EEZ.

75 See in particular Article 234, UNCLOS titled 'Ice-covered areas' which gives to coastal states the capacity to adopt specific measures for the prevention, reduction and control of marine pollution from vessels in 'ice-covered areas within the limits of the exclusive economic zone': see D.M. McRae and D.J. Goundrey, 'Environmental Jurisdiction in the Arctic Waters: The Extent of Article 234', (1982) 16 *University of British Colombia Law Review* 197–228.

76 Articles 17–26, UNCLOS.

77 Articles 37–44, UNCLOS.

78 Articles 58, 87, UNCLOS.

79 1340 *UNTS* 61, as modified by the 1978 Protocol.

framework regulating ship-sourced marine pollution globally. MARPOL places significant limitations on ships discharging oil and noxious substances at sea, and also regulates sewage from ships, garbage from ships, and ship-sourced air pollution.[80] The UNCLOS supplements these specific provisions with general mechanisms endorsing the MARPOL standards,[81] including acknowledging the rights of coastal states to enact laws and regulations with respect to marine pollution from foreign ships within the territorial sea and EEZ.[82] The 1974 International Convention for the Safety of Life at Sea (SOLAS),[83] as amended, is the current international legal instrument that regulates shipping operations at sea to ensure the safety of mariners. SOLAS establishes a series of operational standards for all shipping to ensure safety of life at sea. A related instrument is the 1978 Convention on Standards of Training, Certification and Watchkeeping of Seafarers (STCW Convention)[84] which is designed to ensure certification standards for crew at sea, which is also directed towards maintaining the safety of shipping.

The most significant recent development with respect to the regulation of shipping in the Arctic occurred on 1 January 2017 with the entry into force of the 'International Code for Ships Operating in Polar Waters' (Polar Code)[85] which had been negotiated under the auspices of the International Maritime Organization (IMO) for much of the past decade.[86] The purpose of the Polar Code is to:

> ... supplement existing IMO instruments in order to increase the safety of ships' operation and mitigate the impact on the people and environment in the remote, vulnerable, and potentially harsh polar waters.[87]

---

80 See Annexes IV, V, VI, MARPOL.

81 Article 211, UNCLOS.

82 Articles 21, 56(1)(b)(iii), 211, UNCLOS.

83 1184 *UNTS* 277.

84 1361 *UNTS* 2.

85 The text of the Code can be found as an annex to IMO, *Report of the MPEC on its 68th Session*, MPEC 68/21/Add.1 (5 June 2015) Annex 10; at: http://www.imo.org/en/MediaCentre/HotTopics/polar/Documents/POLAR%20CODE%20TEXT%20AS%20ADOPTED.pdf (last accessed 1 November 2017).

86 For discussion of the role of the IMO in this process see Aldo Chircop, 'The IMO, Its Role under UNCLOS and Its Polar Shipping Regulation' in Robert C. Beckman et al (eds), *Governance of Arctic Shipping: Balancing Rights and Interests of Arctic States and User States* (Brill/Nijhoff: Leiden/Boston: 2017) 107–143.

87 Polar Code, Preamble.

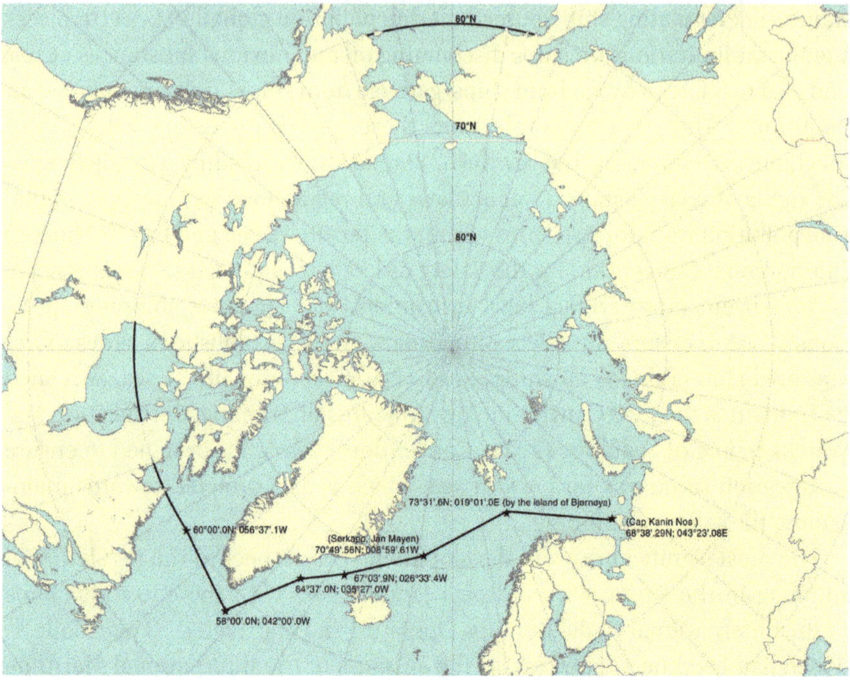


FIGURE 1 SOURCE: POLAR CODE, INTRODUCTION, FIGURE 2, DOC MEPC 68/21/ADD.1 ANNEX 10.

As illustrated in Figure 1, the area of application extends to waters north of 60°N across the Bering Strait and Hudson Bay to a point at 58°N south of Greenland after which waters between Greenland and Iceland are included up to a point on the Russian Arctic coast. The effect is that the waters of the Arctic Ocean are encompassed by the Polar Code other than those immediately adjacent to Iceland.

The Polar Code is divided into two parts dealing with safety measures and pollution prevention measures. Part I-A dealing with safety measures encompasses matters such as ship structure, watertight and watertight integrity, fire safety/protection, life saving, safety of navigation, voyage planning, manning and training. Part II-A addresses pollution prevention and mirrors the MARPOL Annexes. Both Parts are supplemented by 'Additional Guidance' which provide polar specific measures for ships operating in polar waters encountering ice. Presently, application is limited to SOLAS certificated passenger and cargo ships,[88] though there is an expectation that the Code will be

88 Annex, Regulation 1, SOLAS states that "Unless expressly provided otherwise, the present Regulations apply only to ships engaged on international voyages."

extended in time to also include non-SOLAS ships.[89] Enforcement of the Polar Code relies upon the actions of flag and port States, which is consistent with the general provisions found in UNCLOS.[90]

In addition to these particular legal instruments, there remain a number of other maritime conventions that will also apply to aspects of Arctic shipping, including:

- 1972 Convention on the International Regulations for Preventing Collisions at Sea (COLREGS);[91]
- 1972 Convention on the Prevention of Marine Pollution by Dumping of Wastes and Other Matter (London Convention);[92]
- 1990 Convention on Oil Pollution, Preparedness, Response and Cooperation (OPRC Convention).[93]

Finally, it can be observed that the Arctic has in recent years witnessed the development of two new regional instruments which has implications for shipping. In 2011, Arctic states concluded the Agreement on Cooperation on Aeronautical and Maritime Search and Rescue in the Arctic (Arctic SAR Agreement).[94] The Agreement, concluded within the framework of the UNCLOS, is also directly designed to give effect to obligations upon the Arctic Council states found in the 1979 International Convention on Maritime Search and Rescue,[95] and the 1944 Chicago Convention on International Civil Aviation (Chicago Convention).[96] While similar agreements exist either bilaterally or regionally for search and rescue purposes, this Agreement is particularly notable because it is the first regional legally binding instrument of its type in the Arctic. In 2013, the Arctic states reached agreement on an Arctic Marine Oil Pollution, Preparedness, and Response Agreement (Arctic MOPPR

89 J. Ashley Roach, 'The Polar Code and Its Adequacy' in Robert C. Beckman et al (eds), *Governance of Arctic Shipping* (Brill/Nijhoff, Leiden/Boston: 2017) 144 at 150–151.

90 Ibid., at pp. 167–168.

91 1050 *UNTS* 16.

92 1046 *UNTS* 120.

93 1891 *UNTS* 77; see Molenaar (n. 24) for a comprehensive assessment of the significance of these additional instruments for Arctic shipping.

94 At: https://oaarchive.arctic-council.org/handle/11374/531 (last accessed on 1 November 2017).

95 1405 *UNTS* 97.

96 15 *UNTS* 295.

Agreement)[97] which puts into place more Arctic-specific enhanced mechanisms to respond to marine environmental emergencies.

## D *Regime of International Straits*

Part III of the UNCLOS is titled – "Straits Used for International Navigation" – and identifies the geographical attributes of the straits to which Part III applies and in certain cases creates for those straits detailed legal frameworks within which the rights of coastal states are acknowledged and the freedoms of navigation enjoyed by maritime states are outlined in detail. A threshold issue arising from the chapeau of Part III is how a strait used for international navigation is to be classified. The phrase suggests both a geographical and functional element. The geographical element relates to a strait being a body of water which lies between two areas of land, either continental land masses,[98] a continent and an island,[99] or two islands.[100] Yet there is no guidance as to how proximate the bodies of land must be to one another, or at which point the width of the body of water which separates the two areas of land is no longer considered a strait but rather a sea or an ocean.[101] For practical purposes this distinction may not be of great relevance as most bodies of water that separate sufficiently proximate areas of land are referred to as Straits, or have equivalent titles.[102] Nevertheless, the recognition of a body of water as a strait is an important starting point in the application of the Part III legal regime. Accordingly,

---

97 At: https://oaarchive.arctic-council.org/handle/11374/529 (last accessed on 1 November 2017).

98 An example is the Bering Strait separating continental Asia and North America.

99 The Dover Strait lies between the continent of Europe and an island comprising Great Britain.

100 The Cook Strait separates the North and South Island of New Zealand.

101 R.R. Baxter, *The Law of International Waterways* (Harvard University Press, Cambridge, Mass.: 1964) 3–4. George K. Walker 'Definitions for the 1982 Law of the Sea Convention – Part II: Analysis of the IHO Consolidated Glossary' (2003) 33 *California Western International Law Journal* 219 at 298 observes that "The geographic definition of a strait is a narrow passage of water between two land masses or islands, or groups of islands connecting two sea areas". Some named straits can encompass very wide bodies of water such as is the case with the Fram Strait (253 nautical miles (470km) at its narrowest point), between the Arctic Ocean and the Greenland Sea with Denmark (Greenland) and Norway (Svalbard) as littoral States; and the Denmark Strait (approximately 161 nautical miles (300km) at its narrowest point) between the Atlantic Ocean and the Greenland Sea with Denmark (Greenland) and Iceland the littoral States.

102 Of which the term 'channel' is often used as an alternate to 'strait', as in the Corfu Channel; an alternate term which is used is 'Belt. The terms 'Mouth' and 'Sound' are also associated with wide bodies of water adjacent to land within which navigation is permissible,

one of the initial issues that needed to be addressed in the UNCLOS was distinguishing between various navigational regimes that apply in the different bodies of water that may comprise a strait. In 1986 Alexander prepared a US Department of Defense report on the status of international straits in which a total of 265 such straits were identified comprising:

- 52 straits less than six nautical miles in width;
- 153 straits between six and 24 nautical miles in width; and,
- 60 straits more than 24 nautical miles in width.[103]

The functional element is clearly drawn from *Corfu Channel* where the ICJ placed emphasis on the strait being one that was "used for international navigation".[104] While there was no analysis as to what volume of navigation through the strait would be required to meet the usage requirement, reference was made to the volume of navigation through the Strait between 1936–1937 which the Court relied upon in determining that the Corfu Channel had been "a useful route for international maritime traffic".[105] Therefore, while this functional element remains a feature of the UNCLOS, it is unclear as to what level of international navigation is required for a strait to be appropriately classified as an 'international strait'. This is a critical issue in the disagreement that has arisen between Canada and the United States over the status of the waters that make up the Northwest Passage and whether given the relatively limited navigation that has taken place within those waters by way of complete transits that the Northwest Passage meets this functional criteria.[106] However, it is doubtful whether infrequent, irregular or potential use of a strait would suffice to meet the functional criterion. Likewise, the strait must have been used by foreign flagged vessels; and not only by through or cross-strait local vessel traffic. One matter in which the UNCLOS is silent is whether any distinction should be made between surface navigation and sub-surface navigation of a strait. This has some particular relevance in the Arctic due to evidence of

though often these waters lead to an enclosed land mass or islands which front a land mass making complete transit impossible.

103 Lewis M. Alexander, *Navigational Restrictions within the New LOS Context* (Brill/Nijhoff, Leiden/Boston: 2017) 83–118 (this being the 2017 publication of this 1986 work).

104 *Corfu Channel* (United Kingdom v Albania) [1949] ICJ Rep 4, 28.

105 Ibid.

106 See discussion in Donat Pharand, *Canada's Arctic Waters in International Law* (Cambridge University Press, Cambridge: 1988); Franckx (n. 68); this issue is considered in more detail below.

submarine navigation throughout the region, especially during the Cold War.[107] However as the UNCLOS does not seek to distinguish between various types of navigation there is nothing in principle that would bar sub-surface submarine navigation from also being taken into account in determining whether the strait was used for that purpose.

Straits used for international navigation between one part of the high seas and EEZ, and another part of the high seas or EEZ, are ones in which the transit passage regime applies thereby seeking to ensure the ships engaged in international navigation are able to pass through a strait relatively unhindered.[108] Part III of the UNCLOS also makes reference to other categories of straits, including:

a) Straits which are regulated in whole or in part by long-standing international conventions;[109]
b) Straits where there exists a route through the high seas or EEZ of similar convenience;[110]
c) Straits which exist between the mainland and an island where there exists seaward of the island a route through the high seas or EEZ of similar convenience;[111]
d) Straits used for international navigation between one part of the high seas or EEZ and the territorial sea of a foreign State.[112]

Within these straits transit passage does not apply, and in its place alternate navigation regimes are recognised.[113] In that respect it is doubtful whether those straits are properly classified as 'international straits' in the *Corfu Channel*

107 See Katarzyna Zysk, 'Military Aspects of Russia's Arctic Policy: Hard Power and Natural Resources' in James Kraska (ed), *Arctic Security in an Age of Climate Change* (Cambridge University Press, Cambridge: 2011) 85–106, at pp. 91–94; David W. Titley and Courtney C. St. John, 'Arctic Security Considerations and the U.S. Navy's "Arctic Roadmap"' in James Kraska (ed), *Arctic Security in an Age of Climate Change* (Cambridge University Press, Cambridge: 2011), 267–280, at pp. 274–275.

108 Article 37, UNCLOS.

109 Article 35 (c), UNCLOS.

110 Article 36, UNCLOS.

111 Article 38 (1), UNCLOS.

112 Article 45, UNCLOS; this is the case of so-called 'dead end' straits where two bodies of adjoining land separated by a large body of water provide navigational access to land areas at the end of the strait. Examples include the Strait of Tiran, Gulf of Bahrain, and the Gulf of Honduras.

113 See Hugo Caminos, 'Categories of International Straits Excluded from the Transit Passage Regime under Part III of the United Nations Convention on the Law of the Sea,' in

sense. Navigation within those straits within which there exists an EEZ or high seas corridor is governed by the traditional freedoms of navigation found in Articles 58 and 87 of the UNCLOS.

Article 38 (2) of the UNCLOS identifies the physical act of transit passage as including the freedom of navigation "solely for the purpose of continuous and expeditious transit of the strait". This reflects the objective of ensuring that the regime facilitates the movement of vessels physically through the strait from an entrance to an exit point and builds upon the ICJ's notion in *Corfu Channel* of a strait being an 'international highway'.[114] Allowance is also made in the case of where passage through the strait is undertaken for the purpose of "entering, leaving or returning from a State bordering the strait",[115] thereby facilitating ships which are seeking to dock at a facility within a state adjoining a strait, of which Singapore is one of the most prominent examples.[116] Transit passage is therefore enjoyed by ships which seek to pass through the strait, or which are entering or exiting the strait after having stopped at or on their way to a state which borders the strait, and commences once a ship enters the territorial sea adjacent to the strait after having passed through the EEZ or high seas en route to the strait. This does, however, raise issues as to when transit passage commences if a ship approaches a strait via the territorial sea of the coastal State which is not properly characterised as being encompassed within the waters of the strait and at which point the exercise of innocent passage converts to transit passage.

Once engaged in transit passage, under Article 39 of the UNCLOS ships have certain duties that are reflective of some of the elements of innocent passage, though these are by no means as extensive. They include the requirement to proceed without delay, to refrain from any use or threat of force against the sovereignty, territorial integrity or political independence of the strait State, or in any other manner in violation of principles of international law found in the United Nations Charter, and to refrain from activities other than those which are incidental "to their normal mode" of transit, unless rendered necessary by

Tafsir Malick Ndiaye and Rűdiger Wolfrum (eds) *Law of the Sea, Environmental Law and Settlement of Disputes* (Martinus Nijhoff, Leiden: 2007) 583–592.

114 *Corfu Channel* (United Kingdom v Albania) [1949] ICJ Rep 4, 29.

115 Article 38 (2), UNCLOS.

116 The only way in which Singapore can be approached by ship is via either the Straits of Malacca and Singapore, or the Straits of Jahore; similarly for an aircraft making an approach by sea and not overflying the territory of adjoining states, these Straits provide the only means of air access.

*force majeure* or distress.[117] These duties of ships reflect an important balancing of rights and interests within the straits regime. On the one hand transit passage was developed to permit the free and unimpeded passage of ships through international straits, thereby ensuring the continuation of important guarantees of the freedom of navigation recognised in *Corfu Channel*. On the other hand, strait States have legitimate security concerns relating to the presence of foreign ships within their territorial sea in what may be relatively confined waters as was highlighted by Albania's response to the passage of the British warships through its waters in 1946. Balancing those competing rights and objectives has at times proven to be a major challenge, and during the Cold War the United States and Soviet Union occasionally engaged in maritime clashes in incidents which arose from US attempts to robustly exercise a right of navigation within Soviet controlled waters.[118]

Article 44 of the UNCLOS makes clear that strait states are not to "hamper" transit passage and are to give appropriate notification of any dangers to navigation within or over the strait of which they may be aware, which would extend to cases of shipwreck blocking parts of the strait or, as was also highlighted in *Corfu Channel*, mines that may be in the water. It is also made clear that strait states are not to suspend transit passage. Here one of the important distinctions that exists between the regime of transit passage in an international strait and innocent passage within the territorial sea is made clear – while transit passage cannot be suspended by the strait State, a coastal State may temporarily suspend innocent passage.[119] Therefore, even if a strait State has concerns regarding its national security because of the potential for transiting traffic to be caught up in internal disturbances, it may not suspend the right of transit passage. However, it may seek to issue a warning to ships of the potential hazards that exist within its waters at any particular point in time.[120]

The obligation upon the strait State not to "hamper" transit passage suggests that no obligations or requirements may be imposed upon ships that create

---

117 See the analysis in Bing Bing Jia, 'Article 39 Duties of ships and aircraft during transit passage' in Alexander Proelss (ed), *United Nations Convention on the Law of the Sea: A Commentary* (C.H.Beck/Hart/Nomos, Müchen/Oxford/Baden-Baden, 2017) 300–305.

118 The 12 February 1988 Black Sea 'bumping incident' involving the USS *Yorktown* and USS *Caron* and a Soviet frigate is a prominent example of such an incident: Roach and Smith (n. 51) at pp. 233–239.

119 Article 25 (3), UNCLOS.

120 Note that Article 44, UNCLOS refers to "any danger to navigation or overflight within or over the strait of which the they have knowledge", which is a direct reference to the issues that arose in *Corfu Channel* regarding whether Albania did or did not have knowledge as to the existence of mines in the strait: see *Corfu Channel* (United Kingdom v Albania) [1949] ICJ Rep 4, 22–23.

a burden for them. One traditional interpretation of this requirement is that the strait state may not impose tolls or any other fees in return for a right of passage.[121] However, some strait states such as Indonesia have expressed concerns about the financial burdens they face in maintaining navigational aids and other safety and marine environmental protection measures within the waters of an international strait without receiving any recompense and have argued there should be an entitlement to charge tolls or at least a fee-for-service that relates directly to the benefits they provide to international shipping that passes through the strait.[122]

Within the limits of the above obligations imposed upon strait States, they enjoy the capacity to enact laws and regulations relating to transit passage.[123] Yet the UNCLOS is unclear as to the level of enforcement action a strait State may undertake against a delinquent vessel engaged in transit passage. One scenario arises when a vessel is not complying with the requirements of transit passage and its actions are in breach of Article 39 such that it is posing a threat to the strait State or it is not engaging in 'normal mode' passage. A strait State retains its capacity of self-defence under international law and could rely upon that right in the face of a hostile act by a transiting ship. It also has the capacity, consistent with the UNCLOS, to prohibit passage by a ship which is not engaging in transit passage in conformity with Part III. Accordingly, even if the ship poses no threat to the national security of the strait State, a delinquent ship could be prevented from continuing its passage.

Another enforcement scenario arises when a ship undertaking transit consistent with Article 39 breaches the laws and regulations of the strait State. Part III is silent on the actual enforcement capacity of the strait State in such circumstances, which raises issues as to how a strait State may go about seeking to enforce its law in a manner that does not have the practical effect of hampering or impairing transit passage. Nevertheless, Article 34 makes clear that the Part III straits regime does not in other respects affect the legal status of the waters of a strait with regards to the coastal state's sovereignty and jurisdiction. This would extend to the coastal State's criminal and civil jurisdiction within the territorial sea of the strait. This view is supported by the text of Articles 27 and 28 which respectively deal with coastal state criminal and civil jurisdiction in the case of "a foreign ship passing through the territorial sea".

---

121 Article 26, UNCLOS; Satya N. Nandan and Shabtai Rosenne, *United Nations Convention on the Law of the Sea 1982: A Commentary* Vol II (Martinus Nijhoff, Dordrecht: 1993) 236.

122 Mark J. Valencia and Abu Bakar Jaafar, 'Environmental Management of the Malacca – Singapore Straits: legal and institutional issues' (1985) 25 *Natural Resources Journal* 195–232.

123 Article 42, UNCLOS.

These provisions make clear that in the case of criminal jurisdiction there is a limited right to board a ship and effect an arrest whist that ship is within the territorial sea, which would also extend to a ship engaged in transit passage.

If the infraction by the transiting ship relates to a marine environmental measure, other provisions in the UNCLOS will also apply. Article 233 makes clear that ships that commit violations of certain environmental laws and regulations while undertaking transit passage and which are "causing or threatening major damage to the marine environment of the straits" may be subject to "appropriate enforcement measures" by the strait State.[124] The context of the provision suggests that law enforcement against delinquent foreign ships engaged in transit passage is permitted, which by implication would extend to stopping and barring further passage of a vessel to contain any threat to the marine environment. Spain indicated upon both its signature and ratification of the UNCLOS that it also interpreted Article 221 as providing a basis of intervention against international navigation following a maritime casualty,[125] a position apparently endorsed by the United States.[126] Given increased coastal State concern over the environmental impacts resulting from a major maritime incident such as the 2002 *Prestige* shipwreck off the Spanish coast, it would have to be anticipated the coastal States will take a more robust attitude to these interventions in the future.

### E *Arctic Governance*

To conclude this discussion, some comment will be made on Arctic governance which has undergone a significant transformation in the past 25 years. Unlike the Antarctic, the Arctic is not covered by a comprehensive regional treaty-based regime and this has implications for Arctic Ocean management. The first comprehensive effort to implement an Arctic-wide regime was the 1991 Arctic Environmental Protection Strategy (AEPS).[127] The AEPS, which included Canada, Denmark, Finland, Iceland, Norway, Sweden, Russia, and USA, sought to identify existing and emerging Arctic environmental problems and issues and develop action plans for their management. Major environmental problems highlighted at that time included persistent organic contaminants,

---

124 Erik Jaap Molenaar, *Coastal State Jurisdiction over Vessel-Source Pollution* (Kluwer Law International, The Hague: 1998) 295–298.

125 Spain 'Upon ratification' (15 January 1997) United Nations Division for Ocean Affairs and the Law of the Sea "Declarations and statements" at: http://www.un.org/Depts/los/convention_agreements/convention_declarations.htm#Spain Upon signature (last accessed 1 November 2017).

126 Roach and Smith (n. 51) at pp. 292–293.

127 30 International Legal Materials 1624.

oil pollution, heavy metals, noise, radioactivity, and acidification. The AEPS sought to tackle these issues through the development of Action Plans and six Working Groups.[128] This process was never intended to create legally binding obligations but rather to influence collective policy development with ultimate action being through individual State environmental laws and policies. There was also an emphasis on the need to engage Arctic indigenous peoples in this process in recognition of the impact these environmental issues would have upon their culture. Building on the success of this initiative, in 1996 the eight Arctic States formed the 'Arctic Council' in order to provide a high-level Ministerial forum for discussion of issues of common interest amongst the Arctic States. The founding instrument is the 1996 Ottawa Declaration,[129] which is non-legally binding but which outlines the aspirations, purpose and scope of the Council. Importantly, for the current discussion the Ottawa Declaration makes clear that it "should not deal with matters related to military security."[130] While there had been debate over whether there should be a legally binding instrument creating a firm legal foundation for the Arctic Council, and comparisons made with the situation in Antarctica,[131] there has been no significant support for such an initiative at this time from amongst the Arctic States. This was particularly highlighted by the Ilulissat Declaration, where the signatories, albeit only five of the eight Arctic Council permanent members, indicated that they saw "see no need to develop a comprehensive international legal regime to govern the Arctic Ocean."

Notwithstanding the absence of a foundation treaty framework, the Arctic Council has been able to give further momentum to the original AEPS agenda

128 See generally Timo Koivurova and David L. VanderZwaag, 'The Arctic Council at 10 years: retrospect and prospects' (2007) 40 *University of British Columbia Law Review* 121–194.

129 Declaration on the Establishment of the Arctic Council, done in Ottawa on September 19, 1996, at: https://oaarchive.arctic-council.org/bitstream/handle/11374/85/EDOCS-1752-v2-ACMMCA00_Ottawa_1996_Founding_Declaration.PDF?sequence=5&isAllowed=y (accessed on 1 November 2017).

130 Ibid., para. 1, footnote 1.

131 See e.g. Donald R. Rothwell, 'Polar opposites: environmental discourses and management in Antarctica and the Arctic' in Brad Jessup and Kim Rubenstein (eds), *Environmental Discourses in Public and International Law* (Cambridge University Press, Cambridge: 2012) 355–374, Julia Jabour and Melissa Weber, 'Is it Time to Cut the Gordian Knot of Polar Sovereignty?' (2008) 17 *Review of European Community and International Environmental Law* 27–40; Timo Koivurova, 'Environmental protection in the Arctic and Antarctic: can the polar regimes learn from each other?' (2005) 33 *International Journal of Legal Information* 204–281; cf Stephens referring to the "limits of polar comparativism", Tim Stephens, 'The Arctic and Antarctic Regimes and the Limits of Polar Comparativism' (2011) 54 *German Yearbook of International Law* 315–349.

and since its founding has emerged as a body with a real agenda and some notable achievements which Molenaar has referred to as the 'Arctic Council System'.[132] A number of the Arctic Council's working groups have a strong focus on the marine environment, which in turn sees their work have implications for Arctic shipping. This includes the Arctic Monitoring and Assessment Programme (AMAP), the Emergency Prevention, Preparedness and Response Working Group (EPPR), and the Protection of the Arctic Marine Environment (PAME) Working Group. From these various initiatives emerged Arctic Council sponsorship in 2011 of the Arctic SAR Agreement, which was continued with adoption of the Arctic MOPPR Agreement. Developments within the Arctic Council were further bolstered in 2013 with the establishment of an Arctic Council Secretariat in Tromsø, Norway. However, this in turn has raised further issues for the Arctic Council and the role that can be played in these processes by States from outside the Arctic but with an interest in Arctic affairs. The Arctic Council's response has been to allow 'Observer status' to certain non-arctic states, inter-governmental and inter-parliamentary organizations, and non-governmental organizations. A total of 13 non-Arctic states have been admitted as Permanent Observer States to the Arctic Council: France, Germany, Italy, Japan, The Netherlands, People's Republic of China, Poland, Republic of India, Republic of Korea, Republic of Singapore, Spain, Switzerland, and United Kingdom.[133]

## III Arctic Navigation

This part commences with a brief consideration of the principal navigation routes throughout the Arctic before progressing to an assessment of the most contentious of those navigation routes from a shipping perspective: the Northwest Passage, and the Bering Strait. The status of those straits from the perspective of international law and UNCLOS will then each be assessed. Likewise, the status of four other straits within the North American Arctic will also be considered: Nares Strait, Davis Strait, Fram Strait, and Denmark Strait. Consideration will then be given to Arctic EEZ and high seas navigation and

132 Erik J. Molenaar, 'The Arctic, the Arctic Council, and the Law of the Sea' in Robert C. Beckman et al (eds), *Governance of Arctic Shipping: Balancing Rights and Interests of Arctic States and User States* (Brill/Nijhoff: Leiden/Boston: 2017) 24 at pp. 55–59.

133 See Arctic Council "Observers" at: https://www.arctic-council.org/index.php/en/about-us/arctic-council/observers (last accessed 1 November 2017); and comment in Molenaar (n. 132) at pp. 48–53.

the distinctive issues that it raises compared to navigation within the territorial sea or an international strait. To conclude, Canadian and US Arctic rights and interests from a political and policy perspective will be assessed both individually and jointly.

### A *Arctic Navigation Routes*

It has been noted above that the Arctic Ocean has significant 'choke points' for navigation and in the late Twentieth Century this resulted in the spotlight being placed upon the so-called Greenland-Iceland-United Kingdom (GIUK) Gap to monitor the movement of nuclear submarines. Likewise, the Bering Strait and Fram Strait were of strategic significance because of the respective access they provided to and from the Arctic via the Pacific and Atlantic Oceans. The major points of access to the Arctic Ocean are through different bodies of water, all of which are referred to as straits but which have varying legal status under the law of the sea. Those straits and their littoral states are:

- Northwest Passage – between the North Atlantic Ocean and the Beaufort Sea with Canada the littoral State;
- Bering Strait – between the Bering Sea and the Chukchi Sea with Russia and the United States as littoral States;
- Nares Strait – between Baffin Bay and the Lincoln Sea with Canada and Denmark (Greenland) as littoral States;
- Davis Strait – between the Labrador Sea and Baffin Bay with Canada and Denmark (Greenland) as littoral States;
- Fram Strait – between the Arctic Ocean and the Greenland Sea with Denmark (Greenland) and Norway (Svalbard) as littoral States; and the
- Denmark Strait – between the Atlantic Ocean and the Greenland Sea with Denmark (Greenland) and Iceland the littoral States.

The Norwegian Sea between Iceland and Norway provides access to the Fram Strait, however navigation through this body of water is predominantly through high sea equivalent areas and is not considered to be part of an international strait or equivalent waterway.[134] Figure 2 shows shipping routes throughout the Arctic Ocean.

134 Likewise the waterway that exists between Svalbard and Franz Joseph Land is not considered in this study for the principal reason that it provides access to the Barents Sea and not to the North Atlantic other than via a route through the Norwegian Sea.

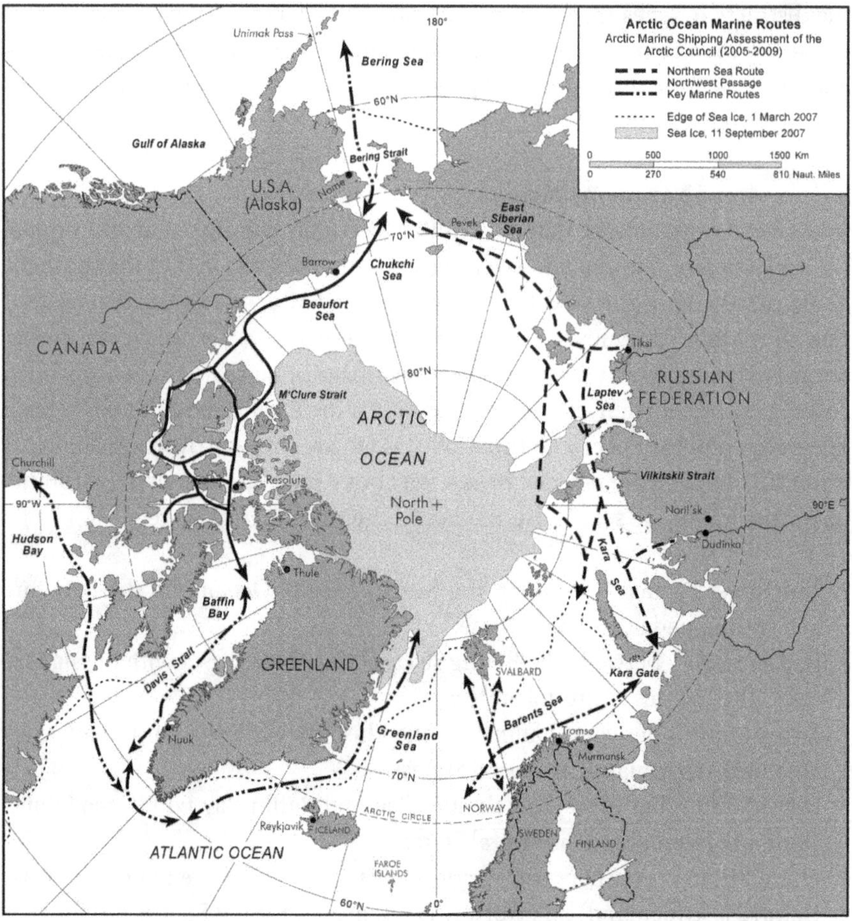


FIGURE 2 SOURCE: ROBERT C. BECKMAN ET AL (EDS), GOVERNANCE OF ARCTIC SHIPPING: BALANCING RIGHTS AND INTERESTS OF ARCTIC STATES AND USER STATES (BRILL/NIJHOFF, LEIDEN/BOSTON: 2017) FIGURE 1.2.

### B *Northwest Passage*

The Northwest Passage is a series of connected straits that weave through the islands that make up the Canadian Arctic Archipelago. From the east, it allows shipping to pass from the North Atlantic up through Davis Strait through the archipelago and into the Beaufort Sea which then provides access to the Chukchi Sea and the Bering Strait. While there are many potential navigation routes that in theory exist within the Canadian Arctic Archipelago, the reality is that historically due to the presence of heavy ice and the shallow draught in some of the straits there have only been a handful of viable combinations of straits that allow for commercial shipping to pass through the Northwest Passage. Pharand has identified seven routes that have been used for transit of the Northwest Passage as follows:[135]

- Route 1: M'Clure Strait, Viscount Melville Sound, Barrow Strait and Lancaster Sound.
- Route 2: Amundsen Gulf, Prince of Wales Strait, Viscount Melville Sound, Barrow Strait and Lancaster Sound.
- Route 3: Amundsen Gulf, coastal waters to Victoria Strait, Larsen Sound, Franklin Strait, Peel Sound, Barrow Strait and Lancaster Sound.
- Route 4: Similar to Route 3, but via Simpson, Rae and James Ross Straits.
- Route 5: Similar to Route 3, but via Bellot Strait, not Peel Sound, then Price Regent Inlet and Lancaster Sound.
- Route 6: Similar to Route 4, Simpson and James Ross Straits, then via Bellot Strait, Prince Regent Inlet and Lancaster Sound.
- Route 7: By whichever route from the west, then through the Gulf of Boothia, Fury and Hecla Strait, Foxe Basin, Foxe Channel and Hudson Strait.

### 1 *Manhattan* and *Polar Sea* Voyages

The status of the Northwest Passage as a shipping route had legally been relatively uncontroversial for much of the Twentieth Century. This was primarily due to the lack of interest that had been shown by commercial navigation in the use of the Passage, and the challenges posed to such navigation by the ice conditions. While the US took an interest in the Northwest Passage during the early part of the Twentieth Century, this was a lesser order issue compared to Arctic sovereignty more generally and ultimately the threat posed by the Soviet Union across the Arctic Ocean during the Cold War.[136] This all changed in 1969 with the voyage of the SS *Manhattan* from the Beaufort Sea through the Northwest Passage to the Davis Strait. The *Manhattan* was an icebreaking supertanker carrying a small quantity of oil that was intentionally sent through the Northwest Passage by its US owners to demonstrate that such a vessel was capable of year-round sailings between Alaska and the US East Coast. The

135 Pharand (n. 32) at p. 29; see also R K Headland, 'Ten decades of transits of the Northwest Passage' (2010) 33 (1–2) *Polar Geography* 1 at 2, 11.

136 Grant (n. 1) at pp. 247–338.

voyage at that time was only the fifth recorded transit of the Northwest Passage, and the first since the end of World War II by a non-government vessel.[137]

Despite the fact that there was a Canadian government official on board during the voyage, and that the *Manhattan* was accompanied by the Canadian Coast Guard vessel *J.A. Macdonald*,[138] the voyage raised multiple issues for the Canadian government.[139] Ultimately it was the second proposed voyage of the *Manhattan*, scheduled to take place in 1970 and again accompanied by the *J.A. Macdonald*, that raised further public concerns about the status of the Northwest Passage and related fears about Canadian Arctic sovereignty. The United States was perceived, rightly or wrongly, as ignoring Canadian sovereignty by these voyages through 'Canadian waters' and public pressure grew for the Government of Canada to reaffirm Canada's Arctic sovereignty and to ensure that any future voyages did not pose a threat to that sovereignty.[140]

In the wake of the *Manhattan* voyage Canada adopted a number of measures including enactment of the *Arctic Waters Pollution Prevention Act*,[141] extension of the Canadian territorial sea from three to 12 nautical miles, and modification of Canada's acceptance of the compulsory jurisdiction of the International Court of Justice so as to place a bar on any attempt by the United States to challenge Canada's actions before the court. Canada's response to the *Manhattan*, which took place prior to the commencement of the Third United Nations Conference on the Law of the Sea, were not welcomed by the US. The Department of State asserted that:

> International law provides no basis for these proposed unilateral extensions of jurisdiction on the high seas, and the United States can neither accept or acquiesce in the assertions of such jurisdiction.[142]

---

137 See discussion of the voyage at T.C. Pullen, 'What Price Canadian Sovereignty?' (1987) 113 (9) *Proceedings of the US Naval Institute* 66 at 69–71; Pharand observes that the USCG ships *Storis*, *Spar* and *Bramble* (all icebreakers) all completed transits in 1957: Pharand (n. 32) at p. 31.

138 Pullen (n. 137) at p. 71.

139 See his initial review see Donat Pharand, *The Law of the Sea of the Arctic with Special Reference to Canada* (University of Ottawa Press, Ottawa: 1973) 55–57.

140 See discussion in Maxwell Cohen, 'The Arctic and the National Interest' (1970) 26 *International Journal* 52 at 67–68.

141 *Arctic Waters Pollution Prevention Act* 1970 (Canada).

142 J.A. Beesley and C.B. Bourne (eds), 'Canadian Practice in International Law during 1970 as Reflected Mainly in Public Correspondence and Statements of the Department of External Affairs' (1971) 9 *Canadian Yearbook of International Law* 288.

Particular concern was raised as to the impact of these actions upon the freedom of navigation.[143]

Further controversy arose over the status of the Northwest Passage between Canada and the US in 1985 when it was announced that the *USCG Polar Sea* would sail through the Passage from east to west as part of a repositioning of the vessel from Greenland to the US West Coast. At the time the US Embassy in Ottawa informed the Canadian Department of External Affairs on 21 May 1985 of the proposed voyage but did not seek permission for the voyage to take place. It was observed in a *demarche* that:

> The United States considers that this transit by the icebreaker *Polar Sea* will be an exercise of navigational rights and freedoms not requiring prior notification. The United States appreciates that Canada may not share this position.[144]

The US *demarche* was careful to state that an invitation to Canada for its officials to be 'on-board participants' during the transit of the *Polar Sea* was not "inconsistent with its juridical position" and that Canadian participation in the transit would likewise not be inconsistent with its juridical position.[145]

Following a Canadian response of 11 June in which Canada made clear that the "waters of the Arctic Archipelago, including the Northwest Passage, are internal waters of Canada and fall within Canadian sovereignty",[146] the US responded on 24 June by observing that it "did not share this view" and made clear that while it was pleased to invite Canadian participation in the transit, "it has not sought the permission of the Government of Canada, nor has it given notification of the fact of the transit."[147] At the time the Canadian Minister for External Affairs, Joe Clark, commented in the House of Commons that the voyage "does not compromise in any way the sovereignty of Canada over our northern waters, or affect the quite legitimate differences of views that exist between Canada or the United States on that question."[148]

---

143 Ibid., at pp. 287–288; see also Marian Nash, *Cumulative Digest of United States Practice in International Law 1981–1988* Book II (Department of State, Washington: 1994) 2042–244; Roach and Smith (n. 51) at p. 319.

144 Roach and Smith (n. 51) at p. 320.

145 Ibid., at p. 321.

146 Ibid.

147 Ibid., at p. 322; see also Nash (n. 143) at pp. 2044–2049.

148 Canada, House of Commons, Debates, vol IV at 6,043 (20 June 1985).

The *Polar Sea* completed its transit of the Northwest Passage between 1–11 August 1985. However, in September and following a comprehensive review of Canadian Arctic Policy, Clark announced to the Canadian Parliament a series of six new initiatives that were designed to clarify Canada's legal position with respect to the region. These initiatives included the declaration of straight baselines around the islands that make up the Canadian Arctic Archipelago, new legislation to enforce Canadian civil and criminal law in the waters enclosed within the baselines, and talks with the US on cooperation over Arctic waters.[149]

The 1988 Agreement on Arctic Cooperation[150] between Canada and the US is often interpreted as being closely linked to the *Polar Sea* voyage and Canada's response. The Agreement focusses on the shared interest of both countries in research conducted during icebreaker navigation off their Arctic coasts and commits both governments to facilitating such navigation and to share research information arising from such voyages. However the Agreement also touches upon Northwest Passage issues and directly alludes to this when in Article 3 it provides:

> The Government of the United States pledges that all navigation by US icebreakers within waters claimed by Canada to be internal will be undertaken with the consent of the Government of Canada.

In the wake of Canada's 1985 baselines declaration, which enclosed the waters of the Northwest Passage within Canadian proclaimed baselines thereby making all of those waters internal waters, any US icebreaker navigation through the Northwest Passage would pass through Canadian internal waters and so be caught by the apparent obligations to request Canadian consent. However as both Pharand and McDorman have separately noted the consent provision needs to be read in the context of how the Agreement was framed around cooperation for the purposes of research and that as there is no right under international law for foreign vessels to conduct research within internal waters of another state, the consent provision became necessary so as to acknowledge Canada's core entitlement under international law.[151] Even if the US had maintained that any transit of the Northwest Passage by its Coast Guard icebreakers was in fact an exercise of transit passage through an international strait,

---

149 Canada, House of Commons, Debates, vol V at 6,463 (10 September 1985).

150 Agreement between the Government of Canada and the Government of the United States of America on Arctic Cooperation, 1852 *UNTS* No 31529.

151 Pharand (n. 32) at pp. 39–40; and McDorman (n. 20) at p. 250.

permission would still have been required to conduct research because marine scientific research is not a right that is enjoyed by foreign flagged vessels in transit passage.[152]

The 1988 Agreement further sought to maintain the essential position of both parties with respect to their prior interpretations of the law of the sea when in Article 4 it was provided that:

> Nothing in this agreement of cooperative endeavour between Arctic neighbours and friends nor any practice thereunder affects the respective positions of the Governments of the United States and of Canada on the Law of the Sea in this or other maritime areas or their respective positions regarding third parties.

At a Press Conference involving Canadian Minister for External Affairs, Joe Clark, and the US Secretary of State, George Shultz, that followed the conclusion of the Agreement it was apparent that both governments were of the view that their positions regarding sovereignty over the Northwest Passage, and particularly the US position as to whether consent was required for transit by US military vessels, had not changed as a result of the Agreement.[153]

The first request by the US for an icebreaker transit conducted consistently with the 1988 Agreement occurred in October 1988 when consent was sought for transit of the USCG *Polar Star*. In a Note from the US Embassy in Ottawa the US expressly sought the consent of the Government of Canada for the transit during which it was made clear that marine scientific research would be conducted. It was also made clear that the *Polar Star* would operate consistently with Canadian law, and a further offer was made that costs incurred from any discharge from the vessel would be the responsibility of the US in accordance with international law.[154] Canadian consent was given for this transit, which was the first of five transits from 1988–2003.

Through their reliance upon the mechanism of the 1988 Agreement, Canada and the US effectively removed some of the public controversy that had been associated with the 1985 *Polar Sea* Northwest Passage transit and the Canadian government's response. However, formally the US government's

152 Article 40, UNCLOS requires foreign ships seek prior authorization to conduct marine scientific research during transit passage.

153 Roach and Smith (n. 51) at p. 325; see also Pharand (n. 32) at pp. 39–40; Nash (n. 143) at pp. 2049–2052.

154 American Embassy Ottawa Note. 425 (October 10, 1988) reproduced in Roach and Smith (n. 51) at p. 325.

official position on the Northwest Passage remains unchanged. A joint National Security Presidential Directive (NSPD)/Homeland Security Presidential Directive (HSPD) of January 9, 2009 titled 'Arctic Region Policy'[155] asserted that with respect to US National Security and Homeland Security Interests in the Arctic that:

> Freedom of the seas is a top national priority. The Northwest Passage is a strait used for international navigation, and the Northern Sea Route includes straits used for international navigation; the regime of transit passage applies to passage through those straits.[156]

More recently, the Obama Administration released the 2013 *National Strategy for the Arctic Region*[157] which focusses attention upon advancing US security interests in the Arctic, developing "Responsible Arctic Region Stewardship", and strengthening international cooperation. The Strategy acknowledges the changing conditions in the Arctic, including that the Arctic Ocean is becoming more navigable which is increasing interest in the Northwest Passage.[158] Under the general heading of the advancing US security interests it acknowledges that the US will seek to:

> Preserve Arctic Region Freedom of the Seas – The United States has a national interest in preserving all of the rights, freedoms and uses of the sea and airspace recognized under international law. We will enable prosperity and safe transit by developing and maintaining sea, under-sea, and air assets and necessary infrastructure.... Existing international law provides a comprehensive set of rules governing the rights, freedoms, and uses of the world's oceans and airspace, including the Arctic. The law recognizes these rights, freedoms, and other uses for commercial and military vessels and aircraft.... We will also encourage other nations to adhere to internationally accepted principles.[159]

---

155 United States of America, 'Arctic Region Policy' National Security Presidential Directive/ NSPD – 66; Homeland Security Presidential Directive/HSPD – 25, 9 January 2009.

156 Ibid., para. III.B.5.

157 President of the United States, *National Strategy for the Arctic Region* (May 2013).

158 Ibid., at 5.

159 Ibid., at 6–7.

The Strategy goes on to identify 'Guiding Principles' which are stated to include "international legal principles of freedom of navigation ... and other uses of the sea related to these freedoms, unimpeded lawful commerce, and the peaceful resolution of disputes."[160]

In March 2016, the US released an *Implementation Framework for the National Strategy for the Arctic Region*[161] which was designed to give content as to how the US would move forward with the 2013 *National Strategy*. With respect to preserving the freedom of the seas, the 2016 *Implementation Framework* provided:

> 1.6 Promote International Law and Freedom of the Seas
>
> Objective: The United States will continue to promote freedom of the seas and global mobility of maritime and aviation interests for all nations in accordance with international law. The United States will promote and conduct such activities in the Arctic region as appropriate.
>
> Next Steps: The United States will exercise internationally recognized navigation and overflight rights, including transit passage through international straits, innocent passage through territorial seas, and the conduct of routine operations on, over, and under foreign exclusive economic zones, as reflected in the Law of the Sea Convention. Toward this end, the US Government will, as appropriate:
>
> 1.6.1 Conduct routine Arctic maritime exercises, operations, and transits consistent with international law. Lead: Department of Defense
>
> 1.6.2 Document US diplomatic communications in the *Digest of US Practice in International Law* published by the Department of State. Lead: Department of State
>
> 1.6.3 Document the Department of Defense report on fiscal year freedom of navigation operations and other related activities conducted by US Armed Forces. Lead: Department of Defense
>
> 1.6.4 Deliver strategic communications at appropriate opportunities to reflect US objections to unlawful restrictions in the Arctic on the rights, freedoms, and uses of the sea and airspace recognized under international law; and to promote the global mobility of vessels and aircraft

160 Ibid., at 10.

161 At: https://obamawhitehouse.archives.gov/sites/whitehouse.gov/files/documents/National%20Strategy%20for%20the%20Arctic%20Region%20Implementation%20Framework%20%28Appendix%20A%29%20Final.pdf (last accessed 1 November 2017).

> throughout the Arctic region consistent with international law. Lead: Department of State
>
> Supporting Agencies: Department of Defense, Department of Homeland Security (US Coast Guard), and Department of State

The 2013 Strategy and 2016 Implementation Framework were both inherited by the Trump Administration and remain current US policy.

This above analysis and review of US policy would suggest that the US position on the Northwest Passage remains unchanged. McDorman's 2009 assessment of the situation therefore remains apt:

> The 1988 Agreement, however, was a political fix and not a legal fix to accommodate Canada while not undermining the US legal position. It is an important and instructive example of the cooperative approach that Canada and the United States frequently are able to pursue to circumvent international ocean law disputes.[162]

## 2 The Northwest Passage as an International Strait

One of the pivotal legal issues that arises in any analysis of the status of the Northwest Passage is whether it is possible to equate it with a single strait, or whether it is appropriate to characterise it as a series of interconnected straits. In this regard, the Northwest Passage could be considered unique as both customary international law and UNCLOS have focused on the situation of a single strait, and not a series of straits that in sum comprise a navigational route from one area of the high seas/EEZ to another. Nevertheless, it is not contested that the Northwest Passage meets the geographic requirement of a strait or a series of straits as reflected in decisions such as the *Corfu Channel* case, in treaty law such as in the Convention on the Territorial Sea and the Contiguous Zone and UNCLOS, or in customary international law.[163]

The most significant requirement, and one that has been the principal point of contention between Canada and the United States, is the functional requirement referred to in *Corfu Channel* that the strait actually be used for international navigation. The United States contests this positon and asserts generally with respect to the exercise of transit passage through an international strait that the right can be exercised through any strait capable of being

162 McDorman (n. 20) at p. 251.

163 See Pharand in Pharand (n. 106) at pp. 223–224; Donat Pharand, 'Sovereignty in the Arctic: The International Legal Context' in Edgar J Dosman (ed), *Sovereignty and Security in the Arctic* (Routledge, London: 1989) 145, at pp. 153–154.

used for international navigation.[164] Pharand's view has been that because of the low number of recorded transits of the strait it would not be possible to classify the Northwest Passage as a 'strait used for international navigation'.[165] This clearly raises issues as to the actual recorded number of transits that have taken place, whether distinctions should be made between historical figures and more contemporary assessments, and the percentage of transits completed by non-Canadian flagged vessels.[166] Pharand identified 15 transits of the Northwest Passage by US flagged vessels in the period to 2005, of which only two were by non-government vessels – the *Manhattan* (1969–1970) and an adventure yacht, the *Belvedere* (1983–1988).[167] More recent figures have indicated 18 transits of the Northwest Passage during the summer of 2010,[168] 30 transits in 2012 and 17 transits in 2014.[169] Brigham has referred to a total of 236 'Complete Transits' from ocean to ocean through the Canadian Archipelago for the period 1906–2015.[170]

Relying upon the actual use of the Northwest Passage since the first successful navigation, Pharand has maintained that the Passage is not an international strait.[171] He has argued that those who contend otherwise confused potential use with actual use and that mere capacity is not what is required but rather actual use.[172] The United States, however, continues to reassert its position that it enjoys the freedom of navigation through the Northwest Passage.[173] Two respected US scholars with close links to the US Department of State observed

164 Roach and Smith (n. 51) at pp. 277–278; 'Senate Executive Report on the Law of the Sea' reproduced in ibid., Appendix Nine, 809 'Understanding 3(D)'.

165 Pharand (n. 106) at pp. 202–214.

166 From the time of the very first transit of the Passage in 1903–1906 by Amundsen until 2005, Pharand identified 69 foreign transits: Pharand (n. 32) at pp. 32–33.

167 Ibid. at pp. 31–32.

168 See discussion in Roach and Smith (n. 51) at p. 478.

169 Environment and Natural Resources (Northwest Territories), '7.3 Trends in shipping in the Northwest Passage and the Beaufort Sea' *State of the Environment* (29 May 2015), at: http://www.enr.gov.nt.ca/en/state-environment/73-trends-shipping-northwest-passage-and-beaufort-sea (last accessed 1 November 2017) ; Headland (n. 135) at pp. 3–9, identified 135 full transits of the Northwest Passage in the period 1903–2009.

170 Brigham (n. 2) at p. 8.

171 Donat Pharand, 'Canada's Sovereignty over the Northwest Passage' (1989) 10 *Michigan Journal of International Law* 653 at 669–670; Pharand (n. 106) at p. 225; Donat Pharand, 'The Northwest Passage in International Law' (1979) 17 *Canadian Yearbook of International Law* 99 at 112–113.

172 Pharand (n. 106) at p. 225; Pharand 'The Northwest Passage in International Law (n. 171) at p. 113.

173 President of the United States (n. 157) at p. 9.

in 2012 that on the basis of the statistics of usage of the strait that "to deny, as Canada continues to do, that the Northwest Passage is not a strait used for international navigation ... is simply not credible."[174] The disagreement between Canada and the US over the status of the Northwest Passage remains therefore a live issue. In recent decades both countries have reached an understanding regarding their respective positions, however as the Northwest Passage becomes increasingly ice free during the summer a point may eventually be reached where if the US wishes to assert its position regarding the freedom of navigation it may need to take a more robust position if it wishes to have its view upheld.

In assessing these differing views, it is important to reflect upon the *Corfu Channel* case formulation where it was observed that: '[I]n the opinion of the Court the decisive criteria is rather its geographical situation as connecting two parts of the high seas and the fact of its being used for international navigation'.[175] The Northwest Passage clearly meets the first element of the test as it is a waterway that geographically connects two bodies of equivalent high seas areas. As to the second element, while prior use of the Northwest Passage for international navigation has been very intermittent, that position has changed in the Twenty-First Century as a result of the increase in the regularity of transit by foreign-flagged vessels. While the conclusion must therefore be that the Northwest Passage is an international strait for the purposes of UNCLOS, some caution needs to be exercised with this view because the enclosure of the Passage by Canada's straight baselines, thereby converting them to internal waters, has the result that all transits conducted since 1985 have been undertaken with consent and not by way of exercise of the right of transit passage. By consenting to foreign vessels undertaking navigation through the Northwest Passage Canada is able to regulate and monitor ships as they engage in passage, and because passage has not been barred Canada has averted diplomatic protests similar to those that have arisen in the past with the US. However, it needs to be noted that Canada's positon has, other than in the case of the longstanding objections raised by the US, not been challenged to date by other States.

### 3 NORDREG

In August 2008, Canada announced that it intended to make what was previously a voluntary Vessel Traffic System (VTS) within Canadian Arctic waters

174 Roach and Smith (n. 51) at pp. 478–479.

175 *Corfu Channel* (United Kingdom v Albania) [1949] ICJ Rep 4, 28.

mandatory.[176] The amendments became effective in 2009 and remain operative as the 'Northern Canada Vessel Traffic Services Zone Regulations' (NORDREG),[177] made under the framework of the Canada Shipping Act, 2001.[178] NORDREG applies to essentially two types of Canadian Arctic waters:

1. waters prescribed under the Shipping Safety Control Zones Order, which encompass waters that extend to a distance of 200 nm from the territorial sea baseline, and
2. various internal waters within Canada's Arctic baselines, such as the waters of Hudson Bay and James Bay.[179]

The relevant waters commence in places as far south as 60°N and encompass the Canadian EEZ as it surrounds the islands of the Canadian Arctic Archipelago to the limits of agreed or respected maritime boundaries with Denmark (in the case of Greenland) and the United States (in the case of Alaska).[180] NORDREG applies to vessels of 300 gross tonnage, vessels engaged in towing or pushing certain other vessels, and vessels that are carrying or pushing or towing a vessel carrying a pollutant or dangerous goods.[181] Vessels entering the NORDREG controlled area are to provide a sailing plan report, position reports upon entry into the NORDREG area and thereafter on a 24 hour basis, and as soon as feasible once a vessel's master becomes aware of another vessel in difficulty, an obstruction to navigation, hazardous navigational conditions, or a pollutant in the water.[182] Final reports are also to be issued once a vessel has arrived at a berth within the NORDREG Zone, or exited the Zone.[183] The scope of the waters covered is such that any vessel which falls within the reach of NORDREG would need to pass through such waters to be able to transit the Northwest Passage.

---

176 'Prime Minister Harper Announces Government of Canada Will Extend Jurisdiction over Arctic Waters' Government of Canada News Release – Office of the Prime Minister (27 August 2008), at: https://www.canada.ca/en/news/archive/2008/08/prime-minister-harper-announces-government-canada-extend-jurisdiction-over-arctic-waters.html (last accessed on 1 November 2017).

177 SOR/2010–127 (10 June 2010) Canada Shipping Act, 2001, SC 2001, c 26.

178 SC 2001, c 26.

179 Northern Canada Vessel Traffic Services Zone Regulations, s 2.

180 Shipping Safety Control Zones Order, CRC, c 356, s 2 and Schedules 1 and 2.

181 Northern Canada Vessel Traffic Services Zone Regulations, s 3.

182 Northern Canada Vessel Traffic Services Zone Regulations, ss 5, 6, 7.

183 Northern Canada Vessel Traffic Services Zone Regulations, s 8. A deviation report is also to be provided if the vessel changes its sailing plan: ibid., s 9.

The legitimacy of the NORDREG regulations were the subject of diplomatic exchange between Canada and the United States in 2010, and between Canada, the United States and other States at the International Maritime Organisation (IMO) at the same time.[184] The US critique of NORDREG is framed around the view that they are not supportable under Article 234 of UNCLOS and represent an infringement of the freedom of navigation. Article 234 relevantly provides:

> Coastal States have the right to adopt and enforce non-discriminatory laws and regulations for the prevention, reduction and control of marine pollution from vessels in ice-covered areas within the limits of the exclusive economic zone, where particularly severe climatic conditions and the presence of ice covering such areas for most of the year create obstructions or exceptional hazards to navigation, and pollution of the marine environment could cause major harm to or irreversible disturbance of the ecological balance. Such laws and regulations shall have due regard to navigation and the protection and preservation of the marine environment based on the best available scientific evidence.[185]

While the United States acknowledged its support for navigational safety and environmental protection objectives in NORDREG and the protection of the marine environment in the Arctic, at the time NORDREG entered into effect the US positon was that they were inconsistent with the freedom of navigation including the rights of innocent passage and transit passage, failed to respect the rights of sovereign immune vessels under Article 236 of UNCLOS,[186] and

184 For discussion of the IMO debate, see James Kraska, 'The Northern Canada Vessel Traffic Services Zone Regulations (NORDREG) and the Law of the Sea' (2015) 30 *International Journal of Marine and Coastal Law* 225–254, at 243–247 noting the views also of Germany and Singapore.

185 Article 234 has been the subject of exhaustive analysis in the scholarly literature, including more recently in Michael Byers, *International Law and the Arctic* (Cambridge University Press, Cambridge: 2013) 185–188; Armand de Mestral, 'Article 234 of the United Nations Convention on the Law of the Sea: Its Origins and Future' in Suzanne Lalonde and Ted L McDorman (eds), *International Law and the Politics of the Arctic Ocean: Essays in Honour of Donat Pharand* (Brill, Leiden/Boston: 2015) 111–124; James Kraska, 'Governance of Ice-Covered Areas: Rule Construction in the Arctic Ocean' (2014) 45 *Ocean Development and International Law* 260–271.

186 Article 236, UNCLOS provides as follows: 'The provisions of this Convention regarding the protection and preservation of the marine environment do not apply to any warship, naval auxiliary, other vessels or aircraft owned or operated by a State and used, for the time being, only on government non-commercial service. However, each State shall

that Canada had circumvented IMO mechanisms through the adoption of these measures.[187] Questions have also been raised as to whether NORDREG is compatible with aspects of the Polar Code and the provisions of SOLAS which create the legal framework under which the code sits.[188]

Notwithstanding these criticisms, Canada has proceeded to give effect to NORDREG within its declared waters that make up the Canadian Arctic. For commercial shipping, compliance is the 'easiest way to ensure hassle-free transit'[189] and because of the exemptions for sovereign immune vessels no issues to date have arisen with respect to US government vessels operating in the Canadian Arctic beyond the Northwest Passage. Much of the Canadian/US disagreement with respect to NORDREG comes down to Canada's history of unilateral Arctic marine environmental protection measures against continued US assertions of the freedom of navigation via diplomatic channels and the actions of the US military. Nevertheless, Canada's reliance upon Article 234 as justification for NORDREG may increasingly be on a weak legal foundation given the need for the waters subject to such measures to be ice-covered for 'most of the year'. As the Arctic sea ice cover therefore recedes from parts of the Canadian EEZ, so too may the legal basis for NORDREG. Canada may therefore have to confront the fact that given its express reliance upon Article 234 as providing an international law foundation for the enactment of NORDREG and given the intent of that provision in providing a coastal State with an exceptional right to adopt certain EEZ marine pollution measures that go beyond the general capacity of a coastal State to adopt equivalent measures in ice-free waters, the right would cease if the waters no longer possessed the relevant ice-covered characteristics. The United States, and other potential user States of Canadian Arctic waters, may therefore be carefully monitoring Canada's

---

ensure, by the adoption of appropriate measures not impairing operations or operational capabilities of such vessels or aircraft owned or operated by it, that such vessels of aircraft act in a manner consistent, so far as is reasonable and practicable, with this Convention'.

187 See 'U.S. letter to the Canadian Ministry of Transport, commenting on Canada's draft Northern Canada Vessel Traffic Services Zone Regulations ("NORDREG") (March 19, 2010)' [2010] *Digest of United States Practice in International Law* 515; 'U.S. diplomatic note to Canadian Department of Foreign Affairs and International Trade, commenting on Canada's NORDREG (July 2010)' [2010] *Digest of United States Practice in International Law* 518.

188 Roach (n. 89) at pp. 161–163.

189 Kraska (n. 184) at p. 247.

position with respect to NORDREG if climate change continues to impact upon the extent of ice in the Canadian EEZ.[190]

## C *Bering Strait*

The Bering Strait is perhaps the most strategically located of the current Arctic 'choke points' given its location at the northern limit of the Pacific Ocean, and the direct access that it provides between the Bering Sea and Chukchi Sea into the Arctic Ocean. Given the rise in Arctic shipping, especially along the Northern Sea Route, the Bering Strait's significance to Arctic navigation will only continue to increase in the future especially due to its proximity to major trading powers such as China, Japan, and South Korea.[191] The Bering Strait will also be important if the Northwest Passage becomes a major Arctic navigation route because of the access that it provides to the Beaufort Sea for ships that are navigating west to east along the Northwest Passage en route to the US East Coast and the Atlantic Ocean. The presence of six commercial ports within the Bering Strait region – three American and three Russian – located to the south of the Strait further emphasise the current and future commercial capability for shipping through the region.[192] The Bering Strait is also recognised by the US Department of Defense for its strategic importance, with a May 2011 Departmental publication acknowledging that:

> An increase in maritime traffic between Asia and Europe, or Russia, could also raise the prominence of the Bering Strait as a strategic chokepoint and heighten the geostrategic importance of the Arctic region.[193]

The Bering Strait is bordered by Russia to the west and the United States to the east and is approximately 51 nautical miles (nm) wide. The northern approach through the Chukchi Sea is relatively wide before it gradually narrows

190 For further analysis of Article 234, UNCLOS and its interaction with NORDREG see Erik Franckx and Laura Boone, 'Section 8 Ice-covered areas Article 234 Ice-covered areas' in Alexander Proelss (ed), *United Nations Convention on the Law of the Sea: A Commentary* (C.H.Beck/Hart/Nomos, Müchen/Oxford/Baden-Baden: 2017) 1566 at pp. 1581–1582.

191 United States Coast Guard, *Arctic Strategy* (Washington: United States Coast Guard, Washington: May 2013) 5 cites a 118 percent increase in maritime transit through the Bering Strait from 2008–2012.

192 *AMSA Report* (n. 25) at p. 108; these being the US ports of Nome, Kotzebue and the DeLong Mountain Transportation System port that serves Red Dog Mine; and the Russian ports of Provideniya, Anadyr, and Egvekinot.

193 Department of Defense (USA), *Report to Congress on Arctic Operations and the Northwest Passage* (n. 43) at p. 9; see also United States Coast Guard (n. 191) at p. 13.

on approach to the strait, while the southern approach has the Aleutian Islands (United States) as a barrier to the east however high seas equivalent navigation through the central Bering Sea presents no difficulties until St Lawrence Island (United States) is reached immediately to the south of the strait proper. St Lawrence Island straddles the southern entrance to the Bering Strait forcing shipping to route to the east or to the west between the island and the Russian mainland. The distance between the southeast point of Cape Chukoski (Russia) and Northwest Cape on St Lawrence Island is approximately 38 nm, while the Alaskan mainland is approximately 124 nm at its closest point, allowing for navigation via a high seas equivalent corridor on either side of St Lawrence Island before the Bering Strait is entered.

At the mid-point of the strait there are two islands, Big Diomede (Russia) and Little Diomede (United States), which effectively create three navigational channels:

- Bering Strait – West: which lies between the Russian mainland and Big Diomede Island approximately 19 nm wide;
- Bering Strait – East: which lies between the US mainland and Little Diomede Island approximately 20 nm wide; and
- The Diomede channel:[194] which is a 2 nm channel separating Big Diomede and Little Diomede Islands.[195]

Bering Strait – East and Bering Strait – West are recognised by the US Navy as international straits for the purposes of UNCLOS.[196]

194 There does not appear to be an official name for the body of water that separates the two islands, other than that the waters fall within the Bering Strait; accordingly for this work it is referred to as the 'Diomede channel'.

195 These measurements are taken from Alexander (n. 103) at pp. 83, 99; the author's earlier indications of distance have been adjusted in recognition of the superior accuracy of the Alexander study, cf. Donald R. Rothwell, 'Canada and the United States' in Robert C. Beckman et al (eds), *Governance of Arctic Shipping: Balancing Rights and Interests of Arctic States and User States* (Brill/Nijhoff: Leiden/Boston: 2017) 217 at p. 222.

196 A. R. Thomas and James C. Duncan (eds), 'Annotated Supplement to The Commanders Handbook on the Law of Naval Operations' (1999) 73 *International Legal Studies* 205, Table A2–3; see also Alexander (n. 103) at pp. 105. To the south of the Diomede Islands is Fairway Rock which is located within the US EEZ, however given the location of the rock to the south of the Diomede Islands and its small size it would not create a separate shipping channel for navigational purposes in the Bering Strait; cf. Paul Arthur Berkman, Alexander N Vylegzhanin and Oran R Young, 'Governing the Bering Strait: Current Status, Emerging Issues and Future Options' (2016) 47 *Ocean Development and International Law*

FIGURE 3 SOURCE: 123RF.COM © RAINER LESNIEWSKI.

The Bering Strait is the subject of a maritime boundary delimitation agreement between Russia and the United States which extends in the south from the Bering Sea, through the Strait, into the Chukchi Sea as highlighted in Figure 3. The 1990 Agreement between the United States of America and the Union of the Soviet Socialist Republics on the Maritime Boundary[197] has as its principal focus the delimitation of the respective EEZ and continental shelf areas within the region and at approximately 1600 nm in length is one of the longest maritime boundaries in the world.[198] The 1990 Agreement mirrors some of the principal provisions embedded in the 1867 Convention ceding Alaska between

186–217, at p. 189; for the location of Fairway Rock, see National Oceanic and Atmospheric Administration (USA), 'St Lawrence Island to Bering Strait' Chart 16220 (2015).

197 (1990) 29 International Legal Materials 941, hereinafter 'America-USSR Maritime Boundary'.

198 Jonathan I. Charney and Lewis M. Alexander (eds), *International Maritime Boundaries* Vol I (Martinus Nijhoff, Dordrecht/Boston: 1993) 447.

Russia and the United States,[199] the effect of which is that Articles 1 and 2 of the 1990 Agreement recognise the maritime boundary through the middle of the Bering Strait, and accordingly reflects the relative positions on either side of the boundary of Big Diomede island and Little Diomede island.[200]

While the 1990 Agreement makes no express reference to navigational rights and freedoms in the Bering Strait, there is clear recognition that while the maritime boundary places limits upon the extent of coastal state jurisdiction,[201] in all other respects the boundary does not affect or prejudice the rights of either state with respect to "the exercise of sovereignty, sovereign rights or jurisdiction with respect to the waters" of the area.[202] It is clear therefore that other than the delimitation of the maritime boundary through the Bering Strait, the 1990 Agreement has no direct impact upon the navigational regime which applies within those waters. The 1990 Agreement has not been ratified by Russia, yet has been provisionally applied since 15 June 1990.[203]

### 1 The Bering Strait and UNCLOS

The Bering Strait meets all of the geographic requirements of a strait for the purposes of Part III of the UNCLOS in that it is a body of water that connects one part of the EEZ/High Seas (Bering Sea) with another part of the EEZ/High Sea (Chukchi Sea). That technically there may exist three geographic straits within the body of water known as the Bering Strait (Bering Strait – East; Bering Strait – West and the Diomede channel) is irrelevant for the purposes of the UNCLOS, and there are many other international straits throughout the world which are formed by two opposite land masses within which they may be scattered small islands.[204] Whether the Bering Strait is one used for 'international navigation' in the *Corfu Channel* sense may have been contestable in the past, but it would appear clear on the basis of current usage that the strait is certainly considered useful for international navigation. For example, the 2009 *AMSA Report* noted that "150 large commercial vessels pass through the Bering Strait during the July–October open water period, with transits of these vessels most

199 Convention ceding Alaska between Russia and the United States, 134 Consolidated Treaty Series 331, 'hereinafter 1867 Convention'.

200 This part of the 1867 Convention also provided for the boundary between St. Lawrence Island and the Russian mainland which passes through a midway point between the island and Cape Chukotski (Russia); Charney and Alexander (n. 198) at pp. 450–451.

201 Article 1 (2), America-USSR Maritime Boundary.

202 Article 4, America-USSR Maritime Boundary.

203 Charney and Alexander (n. 198) at p. 452.

204 Torres Strait (Australia/Papua New Guinea); Singapore Strait (Singapore/Indonesia) are significant examples.

frequent at the beginning (spring) and end of the period (autumn)".[205] While some caution needs to be exercised because of the usage of the strait by previously Soviet and currently Russian flagged shipping, it is clear that on current and future projections the strait will be used by many ships other than those which are Russian or US flagged. On that basis, the Bering Strait would meet the requirements for an international strait under Part III of UNCLOS to which the regime of transit passage applies.[206]

A somewhat unique feature of the Bering Strait is that international shipping has effectively two viable routes through the Strait: the 'Russian route' to the west of the Diomede Islands and through the Russian territorial sea; and the 'American route' to the east of the Diomede Islands and through the US territorial sea. The Diomede channel, at only 2 nm does not appear to be wide enough when compared to the alternate routes to be attractive to commercial shipping. There is also the dimension that the waters between the islands fall within the Russia/US maritime boundary with the effect that shipping would be subject to both Russian and US law at different times as they completed their transit.

In principle, the existence of alternate American and Russian routes through the strait does not raise any significant international law issues given that UNCLOS creates a set of standards that are equally applicable to each route and are not dependent on the strait being a 'one state' or 'two state' strait. It does, however, highlight the fact that the United States has yet to become a party to UNCLOS, and whilst US state practice has been to adhere consistently to the transit passage regime and effectively accept its status as part of customary international law,[207] it still does raise the potential for slight variations in state practice in the interpretation of transit passage on either side of the strait. It also raises the prospect of differing laws and regulations being applicable within either the Russian or US side of the strait, though assuming

205 *AMSA Report* (n. 25) at p. 109.

206 The view is also endorsed by the *AMSA Report*, which states that "The Bering Strait region is an international strait for navigation and a natural chokepoint for marine traffic in and out of the Arctic Ocean from the Pacific Ocean": *AMSA Report* (n. 25) at p. 109; for further discussion of maritime traffic in the Bering Strait see Hartsig (n. 33) at pp. 46–47, 49–52.

207 See United States Presidential Proclamation 5928 (27 December 1988) in which President Reagan stated that 'In accordance with international law, as reflected in the applicable provisions of the 1982 United Nations Convention on the Law of the Sea, with the territorial sea of the United States, ... the ships and aircraft of all countries enjoy the right of transit passage through international straits'; see generally Roach and Smith (n. 51) at pp. 271–275.

consistency with Article 42 of UNCLOS such laws are to be non-discriminatory and to not deny, hamper or impair the right of passage.

Given the environmental sensitivity associated with all aspects of Arctic shipping, some consideration may in due course be given to the establishment of sea lanes and a traffic separation scheme through the Bering Strait so as to facilitate 'one way' north-south and south-north traffic on either side of the Diomede Islands. Such measures would be consistent with Article 41 of UNCLOS, but would require cooperation between Russia and the United States in referring such a proposal to the IMO for adoption. The *AMSA Report* noted there were no vessel routing measures within the Bering Strait and few aids to navigation. Given the significant potential of this strait for increased maritime traffic and the difficult navigational conditions, it would be anticipated that in due course such arrangements will be put in place.[208] In response to these developments, in 2010 the US Coast Guard commenced a 'Port Access Route Study' (PARS) in order to assess whether there was a need to create new vessel routing measures in the Bering Strait.[209] While the area under review only encompasses US waters in the strait, the Coast Guard study does have the potential to facilitate appropriate bilateral arrangements with Russia if those are deemed appropriate. In November 2015, the United States Coast Guard released details on a proposed four-mile wide commercial shipping lane through the Strait, which would also include vessel traffic services and a traffic separation scheme.[210] At the time it observed that 'A thorough Bering Strait PARS, with input from other Arctic Nations, will provide valuable recommendations for the International Maritime Organization'.[211]

208 *AMSA Report* (n. 25) at p. 109.

209 Department of Homeland Security: United States Coast Guard, 'Port Access Route Study: In the Bering Strait', 33 CFR Part 167, *Federal Register*, 75 (No 215), 8 November 2010.

210 Dan Joling, 'US Coast Guard studies shipping lanes for Bering Sea routes' *Alaska Dispatch News* (17 November 2015), at: https://www.adn.com/arctic/article/coast-guard-studies-shipping-lanes-bering-sea-routes/2015/11/17/ (last accessed on 1 November 2017); 'Coast Guard Defines Bering Strait Shipping Lane' *The Maritime Executive* (18 November 2015) at: http://www.maritime-executive.com/article/coast-guard-defines-bering-strait-shipping-lane (last accessed on 1 November 2017); for discussion of potential governance options for the Bering Strait, see Berkman (n. 196) at pp. 205–213.

211 Vice Admiral Charles D Michel (Vice-Commandant, US Coast Guard) 'Testimony on "Arctic Operations" before the House Foreign Affairs Committee – Western Hemisphere & Europe, Eurasia, and Emerging Threats Subcommittees' (17 November 2015), at: http://docs.house.gov/meetings/FA/FA14/20151117/104201/HHRG-114-FA14-Wstate-MichelC-20151117.pdf (last accessed on 1 November 2017).

The Coast Guard study was completed in 2017 and made available for public comment.[212]

These initiatives have the support of the state of Alaska. In 2012, the Alaska Legislature in a report into Alaska's Northern Waters recommended that the United States seek to work within the IMO for the establishment of a Bering Strait Vessel Traffic Separation Scheme in which it was commented that:

> The remote, narrow, and hazardous international strait is located in an environmentally sensitive area with little or no search and rescue or maritime-disaster response capability within 800 miles. Increased vessel traffic in the future will make this area particularly vulnerable to maritime disasters. It is only prudent that basic routing measures and vessel monitoring systems be put in place to reduce the risk of calamity in the Bering Strait.[213]

In 2015 the Alaska Arctic Policy Commission similarly endorsed the adoption of such measures for the Bering Strait.[214]

### D *Arctic Straits and Trans-Arctic Shipping*

To complete this study of the major North American Straits the Nares, Davis, Fram and Denmark Straits are briefly considered. Each provides access to and from the Arctic and the North American East Coast, via either the Lincoln Sea and Baffin Bay, or the Atlantic Ocean.

#### 1 Nares Strait

Nares Strait is situated between Ellesmere Island (Canada) and Greenland (Denmark) and connects the Lincoln Sea on the fringe of the Arctic Ocean with Baffin Bay which eventually leads to Davis Strait, the Labrador Sea and the Atlantic Ocean. At its narrowest point the strait has a breadth of 22 nautical miles, and extends for a distance of 76 nautical miles.[215] The Nares Strait

212 'U.S. Coast Guard Bering Strait Route Study Available' *The Maritime Executive* (1 March 2017) at: https://www.maritime-executive.com/article/us-coast-guard-bering-strait-route-study-available (last accessed on 1 November 2017).

213 Alaska State Legislature, *Findings and Recommendations of the Alaska Northern Waters Task Force* (January 2012) 14–15, at: http://www.akarctic.com/state-reports/ (last accessed on 1 November 2017).

214 Alaska Arctic Policy Commission, *Final Report* (January 30, 2015) at: http://www.akarctic.com/wp-content/uploads/2015/01/AAPC_final_report_lowres.pdf (last accessed on 1 November 2017).

215 Alexander (n. 103) at p. 86.

is distinctive due to the number of smaller interconnecting channels which were named by Arctic explorers. These include the Kennedy Channel,[216] and the Robeson Channel.[217] Shipping therefore needs to pass through the Nares Strait, and the Kennedy and Robeson Channels to eventually enter Baffin Bay. The Nares Strait is the most far northern strait providing direct access to the Arctic Ocean. Shipping coming from Asia via the Bering Strait would, subject to ice, find the Northwest Passage a shorter route, if seeking access to North American ports. Likewise, Fram Strait would be the preferred routing for shipping making its way from the Bering Strait across the Arctic Ocean to Russian, Scandinavian, and European ports. Nevertheless, Nares Strait does present an option for some international shipping, though it has traditionally been heavily ice clogged making it impassable for any form of surface shipping other than an ice breaker.

A feature of the Nares Strait is that the waters have been delimited as part of the Canada/Denmark continental shelf maritime boundary. The 1973 Agreement between Canada and Denmark relating to the Delimitation of the Continental Shelf Between Greenland and Canada[218] extends from a southern point in Davis Strait to the northern end of Nares Strait and entrance to the Lincoln Sea. While predominantly a maritime boundary dealing with the continental shelf in the broad expanses of Baffin Bay and Davis Strait, through Nares Strait the Agreement effectively delimits the territorial sea which in places throughout the strait is only 22 nautical miles in breadth. The Agreement predates the conclusion of the UNCLOS and seeks to reflect continental shelf sovereign rights as provided for in the 1958 Convention on the Continental Shelf, and clearly only applies to the delimitation of the continental shelf.[219] The boundary also excludes Hans Island which is located in Nares Strait and remains the subject of an unresolved sovereignty dispute between Canada and Denmark.[220]

The Nares Strait and its associated channels is clearly a strait for the purposes of Part III of the UNCLOS as it connects one area of the EEZ/high seas (Lincoln Sea and Arctic Ocean) with another area of the EEZ/high seas (Baffin

216 Ibid., at p. 86 lists the breadth of the channel at 13 nautical miles and extending for a distance of 92 nautical miles.

217 Ibid., at p. 87 lists the breadth of the channel at 12 nautical miles and extending for a distance of 31 nautical miles.

218 (1974) 13 *International Legal Materials* 506.

219 Article 1, Agreement between Canada and Denmark relating to the Delimitation of the Continental Shelf Between Greenland and Canada.

220 Charney and Alexander (n. 198) at p. 372.

Bay). It is a strait which is predominantly, though not exclusively within the territorial sea of both Canada and Denmark.[221] However, while the Nares Strait meets the geographic criteria, some doubt must be raised as to whether the strait at this point in time meets the functional criteria as a strait "used for international navigation" given the very low level of reported passages of the Nares Strait since the region was first subject to exploration. Unlike the Northwest Passage or the Bering Strait there have been no significant reports of international maritime traffic using Nares Strait to date.[222] This position may alter over time, but presently it would appear difficult to assert that Nares Strait meets the criteria of a strait used for international navigation consistent with Article 37 of the UNCLOS. This conclusion does not give to Canada or Denmark a right to bar navigation through Nares Strait, however, as the right of territorial sea innocent passage would still apply subject to Article 25 (3) permitting temporary suspension of innocent passage in limited circumstances. To date, there is no evidence that either state has sought to deny the right of innocent passage in the strait. Nevertheless, the regime of territorial sea innocent passage allows for much closer regulation of shipping passing through Nares Strait than is the case with transit passage and Canada and Denmark would find this advantageous.

### 2 Davis Strait

Davis Strait lies to the south of Nares Strait and is principally located between Baffin Bay and the Labrador Sea and fringed to the west by Baffin Island (Canada) and Greenland (Denmark). The breadth of the strait varies from between 172 nautical miles[223] to 510 nautical miles. In addition to providing an access route to and from the Nares Strait, it also provides an access route to and from the Northwest Passage and would therefore be of considerable significance for allowing ease of access to and from the Northwest Passage for shipping en route from East Coast Canadian and US ports. Another feature of Davis Strait is that like Nares Strait it has been the subject of continental shelf delimitation by way of the 1973 Canada/Denmark Agreement, however given the width of the strait this has no implications for delimitation of the territorial sea and there is no area of overlapping territorial sea within the strait.

---

221 Parts of the Kane Basin are beyond the limits of the Greenland territorial sea.

222 Though there remain reports of submerged submarine transits through Nares Strait; see W. Harriet Critchley, 'Polar Deployment of Soviet Submarines' (1984) 39 *International Journal* 828 at pp. 859–861.

223 Alexander (n. 103) at p. 86.

While the Davis Strait is considered by some international commentators to be an international strait of more than 24 nautical miles in breadth,[224] it is clearly a strait within which there exists a very significant high seas corridor and as such is not subject to the transit passage regime but rather is a strait within which the freedoms of high seas navigation prevail. Given the increased level of international shipping – both traditional commercial traffic and increasing cruise traffic – passing through parts of the strait, there would seem little difficulty in classifying Davis Strait as an international strait, albeit one in which the right of transit passage does not apply because it is the high seas freedom of navigation that prevails. Therefore, other than the application of Canadian and Danish marine environmental measures applicable within their respective territorial sea and EEZs, the legal regulation of navigation within the strait would not appear to be particularly contentious.

### 3 Fram Strait

Fram Strait is a large body of water within the Greenland Sea which lies between Greenland (Denmark) and Svalbard (Norway). It provides the most northern accessible access route from the Atlantic Ocean (via the Denmark Strait or Norwegian Sea) to the Arctic Ocean and has the potential to become a very significant trans-Arctic shipping route in conjunction with the Bering Strait. The strait historically is renowned for the large volumes of ice which pass through the strait. Reference to this body of water as being a strait is something of a misnomer, as while there are territorial sea claims asserted by both Denmark and Norway the strait at approximately 253 nautical miles (470km) at its narrowest point has a very significant high sea corridor with the result that there would be no need to for any shipping passing through the strait to in the normal course of events enter the territorial sea. In 2006 an Agreement was reached between Denmark and Norway on a maritime boundary between Greenland and Svalbard concerning the respective continental shelf and EEZ areas. The boundary makes no reference to navigational issues.[225] As Fram Strait is not therefore a strait overlapped by territorial sea claims, and there is a significant high seas corridor within the strait, transit passage does not apply within the strait but rather the normal freedoms of high seas navigation. The result of this would be that one of the two major trans-Arctic navigation choke points would be free of any significant level of 'strait State' regulation, in contrast to the position that applies in the Bering Strait.

---

224 Thomas and Duncan (n. 196) at p. 205, Table A2–3; Alexander (n. 103) at pp. 86, 106.

225 Alex G. Oude Elferink, 'Maritime Delimitation Between Denmark/Greenland and Norway' (2007) 38 *Ocean Development and International Law* 375–380.

### 4 Denmark Strait

The Denmark Strait lies between Greenland and Iceland and like the Davis Strait, does not provide direct access to and from the Arctic which can only be entered via the Fram Strait to the north or if access to the Northern Sea Route is sought, via the Norwegian and Barents Seas to the east. The strait is widest at its southern entrance where the Greenland and Iceland coasts are separated by nearly 485 nautical miles, while at its narrowest point the strait is 182 nautical miles in breadth.[226] As a result, while the Davis Strait has been listed as an international strait for the purposes of Part III of the UNCLOS,[227] the strait is one in which there is a broad high seas corridor of at least 158 nautical miles and there are no significant navigational constraints which would regularly require shipping to pass close to the coastline and through the territorial sea. While it is not therefore a strait through which the right of transit passage applies, like the Fram Strait high seas freedoms of navigation principally apply. The future strategic and commercial significance of the Fram Strait should not be underestimated as it may prove to be a significant maritime highway for trans-Arctic shipping passing through the Fram Strait to the East Coast of the United States, and likewise for shipping passing from the Northern Sea Route across to the Norwegian Sea to also access US ports. Iceland, recognising its strategic location at the entrance to the Atlantic from Arctic shipping routes, has begun to give active consideration to how it may take advantage of new economic opportunities arising from an increase in Arctic shipping, including partnering with China,[228] and an increase in navigation through the Denmark Strait will be an important aspect of those opportunities.

## E *Navigational Rights within the EEZ and High Seas*

The above analysis has focussed predominantly on the freedom of navigation for shipping in the North American Arctic through the territorial sea and international straits, some of which also include areas of internal waters, EEZ, and high seas. While coastal States such as Canada and the US have the capacity to exercise significant controls over ships passing through the territorial sea and

226 Alexander (n. 103) at p. 87.

227 Thomas and Duncan (n. 196) at p. 205, Table A2–3.

228 Arthur Guschin, 'China, Iceland and the Arctic' *The Diplomat* (May 20, 2015) at: https://thediplomat.com/2015/05/china-iceland-and-the-arctic/ (last accessed on 1 November 2017); on Iceland's position generally with respect to the Arctic including the Polar Code see Tore Henriksen, 'Norway, Denmark (in respect of Greenland) and Iceland' in Robert C. Beckman et al (eds), *Governance of Arctic Shipping* (Brill/Nijhoff, Leiden/Boston: 2017) 245 at pp. 256–258.

international straits, subject to UNCLOS, a different situation applies in the case of the EEZ and high seas. In this regard, it needs to be recalled that the Arctic Ocean is predominantly an area of EEZ and high seas and that the freedoms of navigation recognised in Articles 58 and 87 of UNCLOS apply within those waters which commence 12 nm from the normal or straight baselines. Foreign flagged ships therefore have the capacity to exercise the freedom of navigation throughout much of the Arctic Ocean, subject of course to their ability to freely navigate in waters that still remain ice covered for much of the year. This raises for consideration the extent of the freedom of navigation through the Arctic EEZ and high seas.

In the case of the EEZ, the freedom of navigation for foreign shipping extends to the right of those ships to pass through those waters unimpeded, subject to any specific laws and regulations enacted by the coastal State which consistently with UNCLOS can apply in those waters. In this regard Article 58 (3) of UNCLOS is relevant. It provides:

> In exercising their rights and performing their duties under this Convention in the exclusive economic zone, States shall have due regard to and rights and duties of the coastal State and shall comply with the laws and regulations adopted by the coastal State in accordance with the provisions of this Convention and other rules of international law in so far as they are not incompatible with this Part.

UNCLOS here sets up a dual standard for foreign shipping operating within the EEZ:

1. That of due regard for the rights and duties of the coastal State; and,
2. Compliance with the laws and regulations of the coastal State.

Historically there has been much debate as to the extent of the 'due regard' standard and its precise content. At a minimum, it demands that foreign ships operating within the EEZ take into account the rights and interests of the coastal State which consistently with Article 56 of UNCLOS extend to the sovereign rights of the coastal State over living and non-living natural resources, and jurisdiction over artificial islands and installations, marine scientific research, and protection and preservation of the marine environment. Foreign shipping operating within the EEZs of the Canadian and US Arctic therefore need to accept that their entitlement to the freedom of navigation will be subject to certain constraints, even if such constraints are not ones imposed by law. Such an example would be in the case of an offshore oil facility operating within the

EEZ whose presence would have an impact on navigational freedoms within its vicinity.[229] However, there is a counterpoint to the 'due regard' standard that the Annex VII Arbitral Tribunal noted in the *Arctic Sunrise* case where it stated in the context of a Dutch-registered ship operated by Greenpeace International engaging in protest activities in the Russian EEZ:

> At the same time, the coastal State should tolerate some level of nuisance through civilian protest as long as it does not amount to an "interference with the exercise of its sovereign rights." Due regard must be given to rights of other States, including the right to allow vessels flying their flag to protest.[230]

With respect to the second dimension of the Article 58 (3) standard, foreign ships are able to exercise the freedom of navigation within the Canadian and US Arctic Ocean EEZs within the Arctic subject to compliance with applicable laws and regulations that have been adopted by those States. Such laws will be limited in their application by the specific sovereign immunity restrictions provided for in Article 236 with respect to EEZ provisions for the protection and preservation of the marine environment, and by sovereign immunity as generally provided for under international law.[231] In the case of Canada, it has traditionally sought to rely upon measures adopted under the Arctic Waters Pollution Prevention Act post the *Manhattan* incident to provide reassurance that even if foreign vessels seek to pass through its Arctic EEZ it has in place adequate environmental protection measures to be able to strictly regulate those vessels. The subsequent adoption by Canada of a mandatory Arctic shipping registration system via NORDREG is an additional measure designed to promote Canadian Arctic environmental protection.[232] However, as has been noted above, given the heavy reliance by Canada upon Article 234 UNCLOS in adopting these measures, the future capacity of Article 234 to be relied upon may be compromised if the Arctic sea ice continues to melt. In this respect, it needs to be recalled that Article 234 is triggered by "particularly severe climatic

---

229 Article 60, UNCLOS allows a coastal State to declare safety zones adjacent to such installations and structures.

230 *Arctic Sunrise* (Netherlands v Russian Federation) Award on the Merits (14 August 2015) 328; at https://pcacases.com/web/sendAttach/1438 (last accessed on 1 November 2017).

231 See *ARA Libertad* (Argentina v Ghana) Provisional Measures (15 December 2012) (2014) 156 International Law Reports 186, at para. 95, 98 for a discussion of the immunities of warships under general international law.

232 Byers (n. 185) at p. 264.

conditions and the presence of ice covering such areas for most of the year" which on one interpretation is for 183 or more days each year.

While the freedom of navigation by foreign-flagged shipping can be subject to certain environmental measures within the Arctic Ocean, there are significant constraints on the capacity of Arctic coastal States being able to regulate the movement of such shipping within the EEZ. This is a matter that the US has acknowledged in the Arctic context where its promotion of the freedom of navigation for both US merchant and naval ships needs to be counterbalanced against the equivalent entitlements of foreign flagged ships. This issue was highlighted in September 2015 when reports emerged that five Chinese People's Liberation Army Navy vessels had been observed in the Bering Sea off the Alaskan coast. When questioned on the US response, a State Department spokesperson observed that: 'This is certainly the first time we have observed Chinese navy ships in the Bering Sea, but that said, we do certainly respect the freedom of all nations to operate military vessels in international waters in accordance with international law.'[233] This freedom of navigation within the Arctic will of course extend not only to military vessels but also to merchant vessels, and in this respect the interest of China and other Asian States, who have not traditionally had a presence in the Arctic Ocean, must be noted.[234] While access by China and other Asian maritime powers to the Arctic Ocean will inevitably see a reliance upon transit through the Bering Strait, which would see such passage subject to certain navigational constraints under either US or Russian law, once that transit has been completed such ships would have considerable capacity to move freely throughout the Arctic Ocean including navigating through to the Atlantic Ocean via routes that would allow access via the Fram or Denmark Strait.

Finally, it can be observed that beyond the 200 nm EEZ, Arctic shipping will be able to enjoy high seas freedom of navigation which is free of any coastal

233 'Chinese ships headed home after Bering Sea sighting: U.S. Navy' *Reuters* (4 September 2015), at: http://www.reuters.com/article/us-usa-china-military-drills-idUSKCN0R30F120150904 (last accessed on 1 November 2017); see also Helene Cooper, 'In a First, Chinese Navy Sails Off Alaska' *The New York Times* (2 September 2015), at: http://www.nytimes.com/2015/09/03/world/asia/in-a-first-chinese-navy-sails-off-alaska.html (last accessed on 1 November 2017).

234 See e.g. Deukhoon (Peter) Han and Sung-Woo Lee, 'Rights, Interests, Positions and Practices of Asian Flag States, with Special Reference to the Republic of Korea' in Robert C. Beckman et al (eds), *Governance of Arctic Shipping: Balancing Rights and Interests of Arctic States and User States* (Brill/Nijhoff: Leiden/Boston: 2017) 299–317.

State regulation.[235] Once such ships reach the high seas proper they are able to navigate as they please, subject to compliance with general international laws and regulations and the laws of the flag State under which they are registered. However, while the high seas freedom of navigation in the Arctic Ocean may not be subject to regulatory control by either Canada or the US, it needs to be recalled that in most instances ships would need to pass through the Canadian or US territorial sea or EEZ prior to entering Arctic high seas and as such are not entirely immune from the application of either Canadian or US laws relating to foreign shipping.

### F *Canadian and US Arctic Rights and Interests*

With Canada and the US the dominant North American Arctic States,[236] an understanding of how they perceive and seek to advance their respective Arctic rights and interests is important in order to fully appreciate their positions on Arctic Ocean shipping. While there is clearly common ground, exemplified by their cooperation and engagement within the Arctic Council, there are also significant differences as highlighted with respect to the Northwest Passage. Each will now be separately considered in addition to recently identified shared interests.

#### 1 Canada

A dominant theme in Canada's Arctic rights and interests has been the protection of Canadian sovereignty in the Arctic. This has been evident from the earliest perceptions of US threats to Canadian Arctic sovereignty following the *Manhattan* incident to more recent statements from Canadian Prime Ministers such as Stephen Harper's 2007 claim of 'use it or lose it'.[237] Notwithstanding this rhetoric, an objective assessment of Canadian Arctic

---

235 The only exception would be the conduct of an Article 111, UNCLOS hot pursuit following violation of the laws and regulations of the coastal State within either the territorial sea or the EEZ.

236 Denmark also has interests in the North American Arctic with respect to Greenland where it shares a maritime boundary with Canada, however its interests are significantly different given that it is predominantly a European state that is closely aligned with the other Scandinavian Arctic states and Greenland has a dominant indigenous population; see discussion in Henriksen (n. 228) at pp. 254–256 who at p. 254 observes that 'Denmark's Arctic Policy aims at having a peaceful, secure and safe Arctic with self-sustaining growth, with respect for the fragile Arctic climate and environment and close cooperation with international partners.'

237 Stephen Harper, 'Prime Minister Stephen Harper announces new Arctic Offshore Patrol Ships' (9 July 2007) at: https://www.canada.ca/en/news/archive/2007/07/prime-minister

sovereignty reaches the conclusion that Canada's territorial claim to the Arctic has been perfected and that it is globally recognised, with the exception of the very minor dispute with Denmark over Hans Island in Nares Strait.[238] Excepting the Hans Island dispute, Canada's claim to the Arctic has either been recognised de jure or de facto by all members of the international community. Again, with the exception of Denmark in the case of Hans Island, no other state has made a competing claim or could make a credible competing claim to any part of the Canadian Arctic. Any suggestion that Canada's Arctic claim is threatened by other States, would appear to be baseless.[239] How Canada chooses to exercise its Arctic sovereignty is another matter altogether and the Harper government (2006–2015) in particular gave considerable attention to this issue, though not always satisfactorily making the distinction between providing appropriate government resources and developing infrastructure in the Canadian Arctic, as opposed to the very distinctive issues that arise in the context of the Canadian Arctic maritime domain.

The most recent formal statement by the Government of Canada on Arctic Foreign Policy was made in 2013 by the Harper government. That policy was based upon four pillars:

1. Exercising sovereignty
2. Promoting economic and social development
3. Protecting environmental heritage, and
4. Improving and developing Northern governance.[240]

---

-stephen-harper-announces-new-arctic-offshore-patrol-ships.html (last accessed on 1 November 2017).

238 Discussed in C Stevenson, 'Hans off! The struggle for Hans Island and the potential ramifications for international border dispute resolution' (2007) 30 *Boston College International and Comparative Law Review* 263–275; proposals have been made for the settlement of the dispute, see Bob Weber, 'Canada, Denmark should turn Hans Island into a condominium: academics' *CBC News* (November 12, 2015) at: http://www.cbc.ca/news/canada/north/canada-denmark-should-turn-hans-island-into-a-condominium-academics-1.3315640 (last accessed on 1 November 2017).

239 See this author's more extended views on this in Donald R Rothwell, 'Arctic sovereignty and its legal significance for Canada' in Leif Christian Jensen and Geir Hønneland (eds), *Handbook of the Politics of the Arctic* (Edward Elgar, Cheltenham (UK): 2015) 247–261; see also Ron Macnab '"Use it or lose it" in Arctic Canada: action agenda or election hype?' (2009) 34 *Vermont Law Review* 3–14.

240 Government of Canada, 'Statement on Canada's Arctic Foreign Policy' (2013) at: http://www.international.gc.ca/arctic-arctique/assets/pdfs/canada_arctic_foreign_policy-eng.pdf (last accessed on 1 November 2017).

With respect to the first pillar, the 2013 statement asserted the following with respect to the maritime domain:

> With regard to Arctic waters, Canada controls all maritime navigation in its waters. Nevertheless, disagreements exist between the United States and Canada regarding the maritime boundary in the Beaufort Sea (approximately 6,250 square nautical miles) and between Canada and Denmark over a small part of the maritime boundary in the Lincoln Sea. All disagreements are well managed, neither posing defence challenges for Canada nor diminishing Canada's ability to collaborate and cooperate with its Arctic neighbours. Canada will continue to manage these discrete boundary issues and will also, as a priority, seek to work with our neighbours to explore the possibility of resolving them in accordance with international law.[241]

The statement also placed emphasis upon UNCLOS and recognised emerging maritime challenges. It was observed as follows:

> Until now, the Arctic Ocean's inaccessibility has meant that the region was largely insulated from the sort of safety and law enforcement challenges present in regions further south. However, decreasing ice cover will lead, over time, to increases in shipping, tourism and economic development in the Arctic Ocean region. While the full extent of the changes will take decades to realize, Canada and other Arctic Ocean coastal states must begin to prepare for greater traffic into the region, with sometimes negative effects.[242]

The Liberal government of Justin Trudeau, elected in October 2015, has not issued an update to the 2013 statement, but has made some minor modifications to the four pillars as part of Canada's Northern Strategy which identifies the following priorities:

1. Protecting Canada's environmental heritage;
2. Promoting economic and social development;

---

241 Ibid.

242 Ibid.; for an assessment of the Harper government's Arctic policy, especially with respect to the promotion of Canadian sovereignty, see Broadhead (n. 44).

3. Exercising Canada's sovereignty;
4. Improving and devolving governance.[243]

## 2 The United States

While it is indisputable that the US is an Arctic nation given the significance of its presence in the region through the state of Alaska, Arctic issues have historically had a low profile in the US. While the Alaskan Arctic has certainly been appreciated for its strategic significance, especially during the Cold War,[244] the region has generally attracted disinterest in Washington, with one commentator moved to observe in 2008 that "Arctic issues are largely ignored at senior levels in the US State Department and the US National Security Council."[245] Nevertheless, the US has had a longstanding interest in navigation within the Arctic which is not only a legacy of the Cold War and the extensive use of nuclear submarines in the region, but also because of the importance of ensuring maritime access to Alaska and its ports for both security and trade, which in turn are pivotal for Alaska's economy given its distance from major North American markets.

Consistent with the gradual awakening of awareness of the Arctic's importance, US government agencies have in recent years identified the need for appropriate policy responses to be developed as a result of changing circumstances. Two initiatives of the Bush and Obama Administrations highlight the increased significance that is attaching to Arctic affairs in the United States, and reinforces the importance of Arctic navigational rights and freedoms to the United States. The joint National Security Presidential Directive (NSPD)/Homeland Security Presidential Directive (HSPD) of 9 January 2009 titled 'Arctic Region Policy'[246] sought to update US Arctic-wide policy for the first time since 1994. The Policy recognises that the United States 'has broad and fundamental national security interests in the Arctic region and is prepared to operate either independently or in conjunction with other states to safe-guard these interests',[247] consistently with US obligations under treaties, customary

243 Government of Canada, 'Canada's Northern Strategy' at: http://www.canadainternational.gc.ca/eu-ue/policies-politiques/arctic-arctique.aspx?lang=eng (last accessed on 1 November 2017).

244 Grant (n. 1) at pp. 286–288.

245 Borgerson (n. 23) at p. 71.

246 United States of America, 'Arctic Region Policy' (n. 155); Homeland Security Presidential Directive/HSPD – 25' (n. 155).

247 Ibid., para III.B.1.

international law, and the law of the sea.[248] The policy directly asserts with respect to US National Security and Homeland Security Interests in the Arctic that:

> Preserving the rights and duties relating to navigation and overflight in the Arctic region supports our ability to exercise these rights throughout the world, including through strategic straits.[249]

The policy goes on to identify further the importance to the United States of maritime transportation in the Arctic, and the need to develop new measures to improve the safety and security of maritime transportation, including ships routing and reporting, traffic separation schemes, and vessel management schemes in what are termed 'Arctic chokepoints'.[250] More recently, in 2013 the Obama Administration released the *National Strategy for the Arctic Region*,[251] which has been discussed above. This was followed by a 2015 Presidential Executive Order on 'Enhancing Coordination of National Efforts in the Arctic',[252] which seeks to ensure better coordination of US national efforts in the Arctic.[253] In 2015, President Obama also became the first sitting US President to visit Arctic Alaska.[254]

While the 2013 National Strategy for the Arctic Region has been the subject of some criticism in the US for its lack of specifics, including the absence of a

248 Ibid., para I.B.

249 Ibid., para III.B.5.

250 Ibid., para III.F.3; these overarching policy considerations for the United States in the Arctic are also reflected in a 2011 Department of Defense publication: Department of Defense (USA), *Report to Congress on Arctic Operations and the Northwest Passage* (n. 43).

251 President of the United States, *National Strategy for the Arctic Region* (n. 157).

252 Government of the United States of America, 'Executive Order: Enhancing Coordination of National Efforts in the Arctic' (21 January 2015), at: https://obamawhitehouse.archives.gov/the-press-office/2015/01/21/executive-order-enhancing-coordination-national-efforts-arctic (last accessed on 1 November 2017).

253 For an assessment of these policy developments in the United States with respect to the Arctic, see Barry Scott Zellen, 'Where East and West converge: the US embrace of collaborative security for the Arctic' in Leif Christian Jensen and Geir Hønneland (eds), *Handbook of the Politics of the Arctic* (Edward Elgar, Cheltenham (UK): 2015) 550–572.

254 Julie Hirschfeld Davis, 'Obama, Visiting Arctic, Will Pledge Aid to Alaskans Hit by Climate Change' *The New York Times* (2 September 2015) at: http://www.nytimes.com/2015/09/03/us/politics/obama-arctic-alaska-climate-change.html?_r=0 (last accessed on 1 November 2017).

budgetary plan,[255] for the purposes of this analysis there is a clear consistency in the approach adopted by the US towards Arctic freedom of navigation as being in the US strategic interest. At the front line of some of the modern US engagement with the Arctic has been the US Coast Guard, which in addition to having already commenced a number of initiatives with respect to the Bering Strait in 2013 identified the need for improved awareness of Arctic issues, better regional governance, and partnership building.[256] There has likewise been initiatives to try and build greater US engagement in a range of Arctic issues extending from the Arctic Council to the particular challenges being faced by Alaska as it deals with a rapidly changing environment.[257] A common theme through much of this debate has been the need for greater US cooperation with other Arctic states and to engage in Arctic governance. As of November 2017 President Trump had not made any new announcements regarding the Arctic, though it is understood that reopening the Arctic to oil and gas exploration is favoured within the Administration.[258]

## 3 Shared Canadian and US Arctic Interests

Canada and the US have shared Arctic interests which have been further advanced by the emergence of the Arctic Council and the emphasis that it places upon cooperation and coordination on a range of common issues for the Arctic States. In March 2016 Prime Minister Trudeau and President Obama released a joint statement that focussed on a 'Shared Arctic Leadership Model' that placed emphasis on reducing greenhouse gas emissions, working with indigenous communities, and 'responsible, science-based leadership'.[259] The Joint Statement also addressed shipping issues as follows:

---

255 Lara Jakes, 'Critics lukewarm on plans in Arctic' *Battleboro Reformer* (May 13, 2013) at: http://www.reformer.com/stories/critics-lukewarm-on-plans-in-arctic,382452 (last accessed on 1 November 2017).

256 United States Coast Guard (n. 41).

257 See for example Heather A. Conley et al, *The New Foreign Policy Frontier: U.S. Interests and Actors in the Arctic* (Centre for Strategic & International Studies, Washington: 2013).

258 Lisa Friedman, 'Trump Administration Moves to Open Arctic Refuge to Drilling Studies' *The New York Times* (September 16, 2017) at: https://www.nytimes.com/2017/09/16/climate/trump-arctic-refuge-drilling.html (last accessed on 1 November 2017).

259 U.S.-Canada Joint Statement on Climate, Energy, and Arctic (10 March 2016) at: https://ca.usembassy.gov/u-s-canada-joint-statement-on-climate-energy-and-arctic-leadership/ (last accessed on 1 November 2017).

> *Building a sustainable Arctic economy.* We confirm that for commercial activities in the Arctic – including shipping, fishing, and oil and gas exploration and development – we will set a world-class standard by basing development decisions and operations on scientific evidence. Further, commercial activities will occur only when the highest safety and environmental standards are met, including national and global climate and environmental goals, and Indigenous rights and agreements. Canada and the US will work to develop this year a shared and science-based standard for considering the life-cycle impacts of commercial activities in the Arctic.
>
> - *Low impact shipping corridors*: We will work together to establish consistent policies for ships operating in the region, taking into account important ecological and cultural areas, vessel traffic patterns, Indigenous and Northern Arctic input, and increased cooperation of our Coast Guards. The two countries will also work together to share assessments of navigation data quality and capacities for supporting safe and low-impact shipping in the Beaufort Sea. In addition, we will determine with Arctic partners how best to address the risks posed by heavy fuel oil use and black carbon emissions from Arctic shipping.[260]

This statement acknowledges the shared Canadian and US interests in the Arctic, especially in the Beaufort Sea where they each enjoy sovereign rights, and acknowledges some of the challenges being posed by increased shipping movements throughout the region. The statement concluded by noting:

> Canada and the US commit to a regular bilateral dialogue to ensure progress towards the realization of these objectives, to continuing their strong cooperation on scientific work and research, and to advancing our shared Arctic leadership model through the Arctic Council.[261]

It is unclear whether the Trump Administration is committed to these shared Arctic values with Canada, though it can be noted that the US decision to withdraw from the 2015 Paris Agreement is a step back from the high point of the Obama/Trudeau 2016 joint statement.[262]

---

260 Ibid.

261 Ibid.

262 Oliver Milman, David Smith and Damian Carrington 'Donald Trump confirms US will quit Paris climate agreement' *The Guardian* (2 June 2017) at: https://www.theguardian.com/

## IV Arctic Maritime Security

Maritime security in the Arctic is not a topic that traditionally has been the focus of significant attention in traditional maritime security discourse.[263] One reason for this is that the Arctic has not been the scene of the same levels of maritime activity as other major oceans within which maritime security has been a priority issue. This is not to suggest that maritime security issues have been irrelevant. During the so-called 'heroic era' of navigation and exploration in the Arctic between the Eighteenth and early Twentieth Centuries there were numerous maritime disasters resulting in the loss of ships and their crew as a result of encounters with ice and polar weather. In the Arctic this established something of a tradition of search and rescue missions being mounted for expeditions that had been lost at sea of which the search for the missing Franklin expedition in 1848–1856 is perhaps the most famous.[264] By the early Twentieth Century an appreciation did exist of maritime security in the Arctic, but it was very much directed towards safety of life at sea and seeking to ensure that vessels undertaking polar voyages were properly equipped.[265]

The period between the two World Wars had the gradual effect of placing the Arctic under an international security spotlight. While territorial claims were more firmly established, there remained ongoing issues with respect to the effective assertion of territorial sovereignty, which was especially an issue in the case of the many remote Arctic islands that lay to the north of the Arctic Circle at a considerable distance from metropolitan centers.[266] For countries such as Canada this posed great challenges with respect to securing not only territory but also policing the waters that comprised the Canadian Arctic Archipelago.[267] However, it was not really until the conclusion of World War Two and the start of the Cold War that Arctic security entered the current

environautical milesent/2017/jun/01/donald-trump-confirms-us-will-quit-paris-climate-deal (last accessed on 1 November 2017).

263 See e.g. Natalie Klein *Maritime Security and the Law of the Sea* (Oxford University Press, Oxford: 2011) which gives no particular attention to the polar oceans.

264 Grant (n. 1) at pp. 110–113.

265 These issues were further highlighted by the loss of the SS *Titanic* in April 1912 as a result of a collision with an iceberg off the coast of Newfoundland which precipitated the development of the first Safety of Life at Sea Convention: see International Convention for the Safety of Life at Sea of 20 January 1914, 219 *Consolidated Treaty Series* 177.

266 Grant (n. 1) at pp. 193–246.

267 Ibid., at pp. 224–228; K.S. Coates et al *Arctic Front: Defending Canada in the Far North* (Thomas Allen, Toronto: 2008) 42 observe: "In 1920, Canada had had title to the Arctic islands for forty years, and yet had no permanent presence on them"; they go on to discuss,

modern era. The US and USSR faced off across the Bering Strait and more generally in the Arctic Ocean, which given their nuclear capability meant that a missile strike across the Arctic was a possibility.[268] During this period maritime security in the Arctic was a very particular point of focus given the development of nuclear powered submarines with their capability of navigating under the ice for lengthy periods of time thereby giving them access to parts of the Arctic Ocean that were unreachable for conventional shipping.[269]

Given this context, it is particularly relevant that during the height of the Cold War active negotiations commenced at the Third United Nations Conference on the Law of the Sea which eventually resulted in the conclusion of UNCLOS. While the Convention did not have any particular focus upon the polar oceans, nevertheless the inclusion of article 234 in the UNCLOS assisted not only in giving attention to polar maritime issues but also broadened the security agenda to include marine environmental protection.[270] This initiative, coming in the wake of the American and Canadian disagreement over the SS *Manhattan* voyage and Canada's enactment of the *Arctic Waters Pollution Prevention Act*, highlighted Arctic marine environmental security as an issue not only for Canada but also for other Arctic states. This trendline in the growth of contemporary Arctic maritime security issues has continued with the conclusion, implementation and giving effect to of the UNCLOS over the past 35 years.

From a regional and international security perspective, maritime security issues in the Arctic Ocean has fluctuated over time. For the latter part of the Twentieth Century the Cold War had a dominant influence upon how the region was perceived. Not only was the Arctic regularly accessed by nuclear-powered and armed submarines throughout the duration of the Cold War, but during the 1960s there were a number of incidents in which US Navy and Coast Guard vessels sought to assert passage along the Siberian coast through waters considered by the USSR as either internal and historic and through which in its view general navigation rights did not exist.[271] The potential for these regional tensions to have wider international implications throughout the Cold

at pp. 47–49 the significance associated with the establishment of Royal Canadian Mounted Police (RCMP) posts across the Arctic during the 1920s.

268 R. Purver, 'Security and arms control at the poles' (1984) XXXIX *International Journal* 888, 894.

269 See Critchley (n. 222).

270 See Rob Huebert, 'Article 234 and Marine Pollution Jurisdiction in the Arctic' in Alex G. Oude Elferink and Donald R. Rothwell (eds), *The Law of the Sea and Polar Maritime Delimitation and Jurisdiction* (Martinus Nijhoff Publishers, The Hague/New York/London: 2001) 249–267.

271 Franckx (n. 68) at pp. 148–150.

War were self-evident, and arguably Arctic regime development at the time was held back because of this dominant focus on traditional security issues. Only since the end of the Cold War has it proven possible to make significant advances in Arctic regime development and governance. This is reflective of the diminishing tension over Arctic Ocean security between the US and the Russian Federation and the normalcy in that relationship,[272] which is inevitably assisted by their joint engagement in the Arctic Council. Given these Cold War legacies and rivalries, the Arctic Ocean still remains a pivotal zone for international and regional security in the Twenty First Century which continues to grow in significance with the rise of China as an Arctic power.[273] This has had implications for the way in which maritime security has been addressed in the region, because of the historic sensitivity associated with Arctic security and the presence of such major security actors such as the US and the Russian Federation who have extensive national interests throughout the region. As a result there has not been a tradition of much cooperation in Arctic maritime security.

Within the overall framework created by the UNCLOS, Arctic maritime security has been partly shaped by the distinctive regime. Arctic governance frameworks that have developed over the past 20 years such as the Arctic AEPS and the Arctic Council have given little close attention to maritime security. The AEPS, which was inspired by a Murmansk speech delivered by then Soviet President Mikhail Gorbachev,[274] was never intended to address security issues and as its title suggests had an almost exclusive focus on environmental matters which nevertheless in a contemporary context is suggestive of some consideration of environmental security. As the AEPS evolved during the 1990s to

272 An important initiative in this respect, especially as it related to agreed interpretations regarding navigational rights and freedoms, was the USA-USSR Joint Statement on the Uniform Interpretation of Rules of International Law Governing Innocent Passage of 23 September 1989, (1989) 14 *Law of the Sea Bulletin* 13.

273 See e.g. P. Whitney Lackenbauer and James Manicom, 'Asian states and the Arctic: national perspectives on regional governance' in Leif Christian Jensen and Geir Hønneland (eds), *Handbook of the Politics of the Arctic* (Edward Elgar, Cheltenham (UK): 2015) 517 at pp. 520–522 who at p. 520 observe "The Arctic states view China's Arctic ambitions with more apprehension than those of any other state, primarily because of misinterpretations of its views on sovereignty and sovereignty rights in the Arctic." See also Chih Yuan woon, 'China, Canada and framings of Arctic geopolitics' in Richard C. Powell and Klaus Dodds (eds), *Polar Geopolitics*? (Edward Elgary, Cheltenham (UK): 2014) 166–182.

274 Reprinted in T.E. Armstrong, 'Soviet Proposals for the Arctic: A Policy Declaration by Mr Gorbachev' (1988) 24 *Polar Record* 68–69.

blend with the emerging Arctic Council,[275] there has been an ongoing reluctance to include Arctic security issues on its agenda, premised on the historical sensitivities associated with security questions in the Arctic. This is clearly reflected in the Declaration on the Establishment of the Arctic Council adopted in Ottawa in September 1996,[276] where a footnote to paragraph 1 outlining the functions of the Arctic Council made clear that "The Arctic Council should not deal with matters related to military security". As the Arctic Council has predominantly perceived itself as being a forum for discussion of some Arctic issues, thereby enabling cooperation on matters of mutual interest whilst respecting state sovereignty, there has been little support for the development of formal legal mechanisms. Nevertheless, there have been some promising developments that have suggested a shift within the Arctic Council towards the creation of a more legally robust regime. The first was the establishment in 2013 of an Arctic Council Secretariat in Tromsø which has allowed some institutional structure to develop and assist with the coordination of the ongoing work of Arctic Senior Officials and Arctic Council workings groups. The second important development has been the adoption of legally binding instruments dealing with matters of mutual concern amongst the so-called 'Arctic Eight' members of the Arctic Council. These instruments are:

- Arctic SAR Agreement;
- Arctic MOPPR Agreement; and
- Agreement on Enhancing International Arctic Scientific Cooperation.[277]

While these initiatives are welcome, and give further weight to Molenaar's claim that there is evidence that an 'Arctic Treaty System' is developing, they cannot at this point in time be seen as an indicator that the Arctic Council will develop an ongoing agenda with respect to a range of maritime security issues.[278]

275 See the discussion in Timo Koivurova, 'Limits and possibilities of the Arctic Council in a rapidly changing scene of Arctic governance'" (2010) 46 (237) *Polar Record* 146, at pp. 146–147.

276 Declaration on the Establishment of the Arctic Council (n. 129).

277 Done in Fairbanks, 11 May 2017, not yet in force; at: https://oaarchive.arctic-council.org/handle/11374/1916 (last accessed on 1 November 2017).

278 See Molenaar further on the significance of these developments, including the future evolution of the Arctic Council, in Molenaar (n. 132) at pp. 45–65.

### A Post 9/11 Global Security Concerns

Following the 2001 terrorist attacks upon the United States, there have been significant developments in international security law, and the law governing maritime security in particular. Some of those developments have taken place in the traditional manner, such as amendments to the Convention on the Suppression of Unlawful Acts Against the Safety of Maritime Navigation (SUA Convention) by way of 2005 Protocols,[279] while others such as the response to the growth in maritime piracy have been by way of United Nations Security Council Resolutions.[280] Arctic maritime security in the early Twenty-First Century therefore needs to be viewed in this wider context and how the Arctic Council has responded to some of these issues.

#### 1 Terrorism and Counter-Terrorism

In the decade following 9/11 there was a considerable focus upon strengthening existing maritime security instruments that related to terrorism and counter-terrorism and the SUA Convention became a principal focal point for revision. The SUA Convention amendments, including its accompanying Protocol, have sought to encompass a broader range of acts of maritime terrorism including not only the seizure of a ship and endangering safe navigation, but also certain acts relating to the discharge from ships of explosive or radioactive materials. An important consequence of these amendments is to permit a more robust regime for the interdiction and boarding of ships suspected of engaging in SUA Convention related offences.[281] Given the remoteness of the Arctic Ocean and its adjacent seas, and the issues that would arise from any terrorist conduct in responding to such an incident due to the lack of specific response capability in very distant parts of the Arctic, the development of these more robust legal mechanisms to counter potential acts of maritime terrorism are an important development. Russia has already taken some measures to respond to this threat,[282] no doubt mindful of the issues arising from the 2013 *Arctic Sunrise*

---

279 Convention on the Suppression of Unlawful Acts Against the Safety of Maritime Navigation (SUA Convention) of 10 March 1988 , 1678 *UNTS* 222.

280 See e.g. UNSC Res. 1816 (2008); UNSC Res. 1851 (2008).

281 See discussion in Klein (n. 263) at pp. 170–184.

282 Atle Staalesen, 'Terrorism is coming to the Arctic, Putin fears' *The Independent Barents Observer* (December 29, 2015) at: https://thebarentsobserver.com/en/security/2015/12/terrorism-coming-arctic-putin-fears (last accessed on 1 November 2017).

incident and protests associated with oil and gas exploration in the Russian Arctic.[283]

## 2 Port Security

Port security has also been a focal point for attention following 9/11 with the result that a more robust legal regime has been adopted, in which the United States has been a major proponent. Responses to these concerns have included the International Ship and Port Security (ISPS) Code which encompassed amendments to the 1974 SOLAS Convention,[284] and the Container Security Initiative.[285] However, given there are few significant commercial ports in the Arctic, these maritime security initiatives have had little immediate consequences to date. Nevertheless, as intra-Arctic and trans-Arctic shipping continues to develop, port security in the Arctic especially will gain in importance. While the status of ports and infrastructure was discussed in the *AMSA Report*, the 2015 Arctic Council report assessing responses to the report makes no specific reference to port security.[286]

## 3 Safety of Navigation

There have been longstanding concerns over the safety of navigation in the Arctic. The loss of the *Titanic* in 1912 after it struck an iceberg in the North Atlantic off the Nova Scotia coast resulted in the establishment of the International Ice Patrol as a collaborative enterprise engaging Canada and the United States as part of the North American Ice Service (NAIS) which focusses on major trans-Atlantic navigation routes where there is ice danger.[287] The *AMSA Report* identified the significance of these issues to support safe navigation, and critical concerns were raised with respect to the Canadian Arctic Archipelago, the Beaufort Sea, and Russian Arctic waters. Particular recommendations were made with respect to the need to develop electronic chart

283 See discussion in Alex G. Oude Elferink, 'The Arctic Sunrise incident: a multi-faceted law of the sea case with a human rights dimension' (2014) 29 *International Journal of Marine and Coastal Law* 244–289.

284 Being amendments adopted at the Conference of Contracting Governments to the SOLAS Convention, and including the International Ship and Port Facility Security Code (ISPS Code) of 12 December 2002, [2004] Australian Treaty Series 29.

285 See discussion in Klein (n. 263) at pp. 157–169.

286 Arctic Council, *Status on Implementation of the AMSA 2009 Report Recommendations* (April 2015) at: https://pame.is/images/03_Projects/AMSA/AMSA_Documents/Progress_Reports/AMSArecommendations2015_Web.pdf (last accessed on 1 November 2017).

287 The treaty-based framework under which this service operates is the Agreement relating to financial support of the North American ice patrol of 4 January 1956, 256 *UNTS* 171.

display and information systems.[288] A number of initiatives have been taken to respond to the *AMSA Report* recommendations, including enhanced Arctic Council engagement with the IMO (which took a lead role in coordinating negotiation of the Polar Code), developing and improving hydrographic and bathymetric data, and developing voluntary, non-binding best practice guidelines for Arctic marine tourism to advance sustainable economic development and environmental conservation.[289]

## 4 Maritime Search and Rescue

Closely related to the safety of navigation are the associated challenges of maritime search and rescue which were also highlighted in the *AMSA Report*. While navigation through the Arctic has always been extremely hazardous, as a result of the effects of climate change, globalization, and enhanced navigational capability for many different types of vessels, the Arctic Ocean is now being visited by more types of shipping than ever before. This upward surge in maritime traffic – in both traditional commercial maritime traffic and also cruise ships – can only be expected to continue, resulting in concerns about the capacity of Arctic States to individually respond to maritime emergencies. In the Arctic, the Arctic SAR Agreement is an important step forward in coordinating response capacity to better address search and rescue issues. The Arctic SAR Agreement seeks to supplement and build upon individual and collective obligations of the Arctic States under the 1979 Convention on Maritime Search and Rescue,[290] so in that sense it sits within the framework of obligations created by that convention. Search and rescue regions are designated, though care is taken to ensure that in doing so the delimitation of maritime boundaries, or the sovereignty or sovereign rights of the parties are not prejudiced.[291] 'Rescue Coordination Centers' are designated and consistently with the SAR Convention and the Chicago Convention (relating to aeronautical search and rescue) take the lead in coordinating search and rescue, including the use of multiple assets. That the agreement sought to address both maritime and aeronautical response capacity highlighted the need for multi-asset response capability and should pave the way for enhanced cooperation between the Arctic states.

---

288 *AMSA Report* (n. 25) at p. 186.

289 Arctic Council, Status on Implementation of the AMSA 2009 Report Recommendations (n. 286) at pp. 4–7.

290 1405 *UNTS* 97; hereinafter SAR Convention.

291 Article 3, Arctic SAR Agreement.

## V Concluding Remarks

In the past decade the Arctic has moved from the far recesses of international affairs to the mainstream. Debates have emerged as to the geopolitical importance of the region,[292] its governance, and its economic future.[293] The Arctic has also emerged as the yardstick against which climate change is increasingly measured. In that respect particular attention has been paid to the disappearance of the Arctic ice cap, and its impact for the central Arctic Ocean with respect to trans-Arctic shipping and coastal shipping.[294] These developments have focussed attention upon the legal regime in the Arctic, and especially that with respect to the maritime Arctic as this is where the region is seen as having immediate potential as new shipping routes are opened in response to regional and global trading demands. However, far from being unregulated the reality is that there already exists a significant body of international law dealing with Arctic shipping. The relevant international law, principally founded upon the international law of the sea, has not recently emerged but rather has been developed over many centuries and as embodied in the UNCLOS represents the culmination of developed state practice, decisions of international courts, and prior treaties. The foundational law of the sea principles are supported by a number of parallel conventional regimes dealing with marine pollution, safety of life at sea, and shipping regulatory standards. Yet, this body of international law is not static, and remains under development through new initiatives such as the Polar Code.

With the evidence only increasing that a return to previous climate conditions in the Arctic is unlikely in the short term and that the trend to warming in the region is continuing,[295] there is every prospect that this previously

292 Borgerson (n. 23).

293 The Economist, 'Special Report: The Arctic' (June 16, 2012) *The Economist* 403 (8789); at: https://www.economist.com/blogs/babbage/2012/06/cold-comfort (last accessed on 1 November 2017).

294 See e.g. Brigham (n. 2) at pp. 11–12; Joshua H. Ho, 'The Arctic Meltdown and Its Implications for Ports and Shipping in Asia' in James Kraska (ed), *Arctic Security in an Age of Climate Change* (Cambridge University Press, Cambridge: 2011) 33–43; Bjorn Gunnarsson, 'The Future of Arctic Marine Operations and Shipping Logistics' in Oran R. Young, Jong Deog Kim and Yoon Hyung Kim (eds), *The Arctic in World Affairs* (Korea Maritime Institute/East-West Centre, Seoul/Honolulu: 2013) 37–61; Andrew E. Kramer, 'Polar thaw opens shortcut for Russian gas; New shipping lanes ease access to Chinese market for energy companies' (9 July 2013) *International Herald Tribune* 14.

295 See J. Richter-Menge, J.E. Overland, J. Mathis, 'Arctic Report Card: Update for 2016' (December 6, 2016) at: http://www.arctic.noaa.gov/Report-Card/Report-Card-2016/

inhospitable region for regular maritime traffic may gradually become more accessible to shipping with the result that the North American Arctic shipping routes discussed above will become of greater significance to navigation to and from the Arctic. These changes will in all probability take place gradually and whilst there is increasing evidence of Arctic shipping taking place, much remains to occur before there is truly significant maritime activity throughout the region. Some of these variables will includes economics (both global and regional), scheduling, cargo selection, port and infrastructure development,[296] regulatory futures, insurance, and the variability of the sea ice operating environment.[297] While on current projections the Arctic will become more navigable, it will not become entirely ice free, and as Brigham has observed "A key question for ships operating on longer Arctic seasons, when a significant sea ice cover remains, is whether they will be capable of independent sea ice operations or will they require icebreakers for escort or convoy."[298] A critical point therefore is that whilst North American Arctic shipping has considerable potential, there remain significant variables before the Arctic Ocean becomes in any way equivalent to other maritime domains where commercial shipping operations regularly take place. This is to be contrasted with intra-Arctic shipping, especially along the Northern Sea Route, which is already showing signs

ArtMID/5022/ArticleID/270/Executive-Summary (last accessed on 1 November 2017) who wrote: 'Though no new record was set, the September 2016 Arctic sea ice minimum extent tied with 2007 for the second lowest value in the satellite record, at 33% lower than the 1981–2010 average. The sea ice cover continues to be relatively young and thin. In March 2016, multiyear ice (more than 1 year old) and first-year ice were 22% and 78% of the ice cover, respectively, compared to 45% and 55% in 1985. As the sea ice retreats more extensively in the summer, previously ice-covered water is exposed to more solar radiation. As a result, sea surface temperature (SST) and upper ocean temperatures are increasing throughout much of the Arctic Ocean and adjacent seas. Also contributing to the increase in SST are regional air temperatures and influx of warmer water from the North Atlantic and Pacific Oceans. The Chukchi Sea, northwest of Alaska, and eastern Baffin Bay, off west Greenland, have the largest warming trends: ~0.5° C per decade since 1982. In August 2016, SST was up to 5° C higher than the 1982–2010 average in regions of the Barents and Chukchi seas and off the east and west coasts of Greenland.'

296 See especially Chircop (n. 24) at p. 378 discussing the 'infrastructure challenge' with Arctic shipping.

297 Lawson Brigham, 'Navigating the New Maritime Arctic' (May 2009) 135 (5) (No 1275) *Proceedings US Naval Institute* 42, at p. 45; see also Chircop (n. 24) at p. 359 commenting on the perception that the Arctic will be totally ice-free that "More realistic is the expectation that a ship navigating in the Arctic can encounter a mixture of open water and different ice regimes."

298 Brigham (n. 297) at p. 45.

of commercial development,[299] which does have implications for the Bering Strait given its proximity to Asian markets.

Alongside these uncertainties sits the UNCLOS which is already established and operating, especially as it applies to navigational rights and freedoms which is one of the most well established areas of the modern law of the sea. While the Arctic Ocean may therefore be undergoing significant change, the core legal regime that will regulate North American Arctic shipping routes is already in place. While there is the potential for the status of certain straits to be modified in light of increased levels of international shipping through those waters, the legal regime is robust enough to deal with those developments. That does not imply that some Arctic States may not wish to build upon the legal framework of the UNCLOS and adjust it to the particular circumstances that may apply within Arctic shipping routes as has been done in other major shipping routes throughout the world,[300] however this remains entirely possible within the UNCLOS subject to the cooperation of both user States and the Arctic coastal States.

With the UNCLOS at the centre of the Arctic shipping legal regime, two critical issues have emerged in recent years. The first is that whilst the United States has not formally adopted the UNCLOS by way of accession, it maintains the position that it adheres to the Convention and seeks to uphold its obligations whilst also enjoying its rights. In this respect the United States position vis-à-vis the Northwest Passage, where it asserts certain rights, and the Bering Strait, where it acknowledges its obligations, highlights the position faced by the United States with respect to the law of the sea and these pivotal Arctic shipping routes. The second is that by accepting the Arctic Ocean is also subject to the same navigational rights and freedoms for shipping as other oceans it follows that these are rights which can be enjoyed by the ships of all states. This means that states that have not traditionally had a strong Arctic presence will be able to enjoy navigational rights and freedoms throughout the Arctic. In particular, states such as China, Japan and South Korea will all be able to gain access to Arctic shipping routes and enjoy recognised freedoms of navigation. While this development may raise issues, what can be confidently asserted is that the international law with respect to Arctic shipping is well developed and sufficiently robust to be able to withstand whatever testing times it may be facing.

---

299 See generally Jan Solski, 'Russia' in Robert C. Beckman et al (eds), *Governance of Arctic Shipping* (Brill/Nijhoff, Leiden/Boston: 2017) 173–216.

300 Cooperative arrangements which have been put in place between Indonesia, Malaysia and Singapore to regulate the Straits of Malacca and Singapore are a prominent example.

Notwithstanding the US ambivalence with respect to UNCLOS, it remains the world's premier maritime power, and as an Arctic State it has a significant capacity to influence the direction of how the law develops with respect to Arctic shipping, and especially in the North American Arctic. Any analysis of US policy and its legal response to navigational issues in the Arctic needs to be read against the backdrop of the US Freedom of Navigation (FON) Program which has been in place since 1979. As summed up by Roach and Smith, the FON program aims "to preserve and protect the global mobility of US forces, and the navigation and overflight rights of all ocean users. Peaceful rather than provocative in intent, it impartially rejects excessive maritime claims of allied, friendly, neutral and unfriendly States alike."[301] This somewhat explains the ongoing US position regarding the freedom of navigation in the Northwest Passage and that the US has been unflinching in its continued assertions of the right of transit passage in those waters. Nevertheless, irrespective of whether the customary international law recognised in the *Corfu Channel* case, or the provisions of the Convention on the Territorial Sea and Contiguous Zone, or the UNCLOS apply, there is room for differing views as to whether the Northwest Passage is an international strait. It is arguable that different standards apply to the interpretation and application of international law in the polar regions when compared to more temperate lands and oceans.[302] The consequence of such an approach would be that when the presence of ice in the waters of the Passage is taken into account plus the weather variables associated with Arctic navigation, a lower volume of international navigation than would be normally required may establish the Northwest Passage as an international Strait. By way of contrast the US in its management of the Bering Strait accepts the right of transit passage, is mindful of its international obligations as a littoral state while also balancing those against environmental concerns and those of indigenous Alaskans, and is mindful that as it shares the Bering Strait with Russia that there may eventually be a need to cooperate with its neighbour to achieve effective management of shipping through the strait. The developing US experience in managing the Bering Strait may also allow it to better appreciate some of the considerations that have influenced Canadian law and policy with respect to the Arctic and the Northwest Passage for many decades.

For the Canadian Arctic these are challenging times as the region is effectively undergoing a process of globalisation through its opening up to the

301 Roach and Smith (n. 51) at p. 637.

302 See *Legal Status of Eastern Greenland* (Denmark v Norway) [1933] PCIJ Rep (Ser. A/B) No. 53, 46.

world. Suggestions that Canadian sovereignty over the Arctic is threatened by these developments are misplaced. Canada's Arctic sovereignty is as well established, managed and regulated as any of the other Arctic states. It is firmly rooted in international law, both with respect to the international law of territoriality and that dealing with maritime claims. Canada's Arctic sovereign rights will also more than likely expand in the future following recommendations from the Commission on the Limits of the Continental Shelf and the eventual proclamation of a continental shelf beyond the 200 nm limit in parts of the Canadian Arctic. However, while international law gives to Canada considerable rights over the Arctic it also confers certain responsibilities, one of which is to recognise the navigational rights of foreign vessels throughout Canadian waters, including the territorial sea and EEZ. As the Arctic therefore continues to feel the effects of climate change and the Arctic Ocean becomes more accessible, Canada will at a minimum have to reconcile itself with the presence of foreign vessels within its EEZ which providing they lawfully conduct themselves should be permitted to pass without interference. Such a response, however, would be consistent with Canada's position of recognising the importance of international law and acting as a good international law citizen.

Canada and the United States are two of the most significant Arctic maritime powers. They assume this position due to the size of their Arctic lands, length of their Arctic coastlines, the significance of the straits and passages over which they exercise jurisdiction, their historical and contemporary interest in Arctic shipping, their contribution to Arctic governance on maritime matters at both global and regional forums, and in the case of the United States its role as a superpower. Much of the discourse about Canadian and US maritime interests in the Arctic has been dominated by their differing positions with respect to the Northwest Passage. Those differences have been framed around different perspectives on Arctic sovereignty, environmental protection, and the freedom of navigation. While the Northwest Passage has been at the centre of those differences, attention will increasingly turn to how EEZ navigation may be subject to traditional coastal State regulation. To date, however, it is the Bering Strait that has been the subject of significant international shipping within the North American Arctic.

Through a combination of climate change resulting in melting of the Arctic sea ice cover which in turn will make the Arctic Ocean more accessible to shipping of all types, and the interest of states that traditionally have not had a presence in the Arctic of using Arctic waterways as navigational routes, Arctic shipping is on the brink of very significant activity within the North American Arctic. This will inevitably create its own tensions for Canada and the United States as they adjust to these changed circumstances and reflect upon their previous practices developed at a time when the demands of maritime traffic were not as great. There may be different responses emerging from Canada and the United States to these developments. This will partly be the case due to their different maritime domains, different national Arctic political discourses, and different global agendas. The election of President Donald Trump in the US also creates a wildcard given the apparent position of the Trump administration towards matters such as climate change, environmental protection, and existing international agreements. Above these debates sits UNCLOS and related international maritime law regarding marine pollution and shipping regulation that creates parameters to regulatory ambition. In this regard, unilateral acts, which have characterised previous national responses in the Arctic, are subject to greater constraints which in turn should give the international community more confidence on how Canada and the United States will respond to the new dynamics of Arctic shipping.

## References

'Chinese ships headed home after Bering Sea sighting: U.S. Navy' *Reuters* (4 September 2015), at: http://www.reuters.com/article/us-usa-china-military-drills-idUSKCN0R30F120150904 (last accessed on 1 November 2017).

'Coast Guard Defines Bering Strait Shipping Lane' *The Maritime Executive* (18 November 2015) at: http://www.maritime-executive.com/article/coast-guard-defines-bering-strait-shipping-lane (last accessed on 1 November 2017).

'Prime Minister Harper Announces Government of Canada Will Extend Jurisdiction over Arctic Waters' Government of Canada News Release – Office of the Prime Minister (27 August 2008), at: https://www.canada.ca/en/news/archive/2008/08/prime-minister-harper-announces-government-canada-extend-jurisdiction-over-arctic-waters.html (last accessed on 1 November 2017).

'Special Report: The Arctic' *The Economist* June 16th–22nd 2012.

'U.S. Coast Guard Bering Strait Route Study Available' *The Maritime Executive* (1 March 2017) at: https://www.maritime-executive.com/article/us-coast-guard-bering-strait-route-study-available (last accessed on 1 November 2017).

Alexander, Lewis M., *Navigational Restrictions within the New LOS Context* (Brill/Nijhoff, Leiden/Boston: 2017).

Alfredsson, Gudmundur, 'Arctic governance: Human Rights, Good Governance and Democracy' (2012) 4 *The Yearbook of Polar Law* 141–153.

Arctic Council, *Arctic Marine Shipping Assessment 2009 Report* (Arctic Council, Tromsø: 2009).

Armstrong, T.E., 'Soviet Proposals for the Arctic: A Policy Declaration by Mr Gorbachev' (1988) 24 *Polar Record* 68–69.

Auburn, F.M., *Antarctic Law and Politics* (Croom Helm, London: 1982).

Bannelier, Karine, Theodore Christakis, and Sarah Heathcote (eds), *The ICJ and the Evolution of International Law: The enduring impact of the Corfu Channel case* (Routledge, New York: 2012).

Baxter, R.R., *The Law of International Waterways* (Harvard University Press, Cambridge, Mass.: 1964).

Beesley, J.A. and C.B. Bourne (eds), 'Canadian Practice in International Law during 1970 as Reflected Mainly in Public Correspondence and Statements of the Department of External Affairs' (1971) 9 *Canadian Yearbook of International Law* 288.

Berkman, Paul Arthur, Alexander N Vylegzhanin and Oran R Young, 'Governing the Bering Strait: Current Status, Emerging Issues and Future Options' (2016) 47 *Ocean Development and International Law* 186–217.

Borgerson, Scott G., 'Arctic Meltdown: The Economic and Security Implications of Global Warming' (2008) 87 *Foreign Affairs* 63–77.

Brigham, Lawson W. 'The Changing Maritime Arctic and New Maritime Operations' in Robert C. Beckman et al (eds), *Governance of Arctic Shipping* (Brill/Nijhoff, Leiden/Boston: 2017) 3–23.

Brigham, Lawson, 'Navigating the New Maritime Arctic' (May 2009) 135 (5) (No 1275) *Proceedings US Naval Institute* 42.

Broadhead, Lee-Anne, 'Canadian sovereignty verses northern security: the case for updating our mental map of the Arctic' in Leif Christian Jensen and Geir Hønneland (eds), *Handbook of the Politics of the Arctic* (Edward Elgar, Cheltenham, UK: 2015) 281–297.

Brubaker, R.D., *The Russian Arctic Straits* (Martinus Nijhoff, Leiden: 2005).

Brüel, Erik, *International Straits* Vol II (Sweet & Maxwell, London: 1947).

Byers, Michael and Suzanne Lalonde, 'Who controls the Northwest Passage?' (2009) 42 *Vanderbilt Journal of Transnational Law* 1133–1210.

Byers, Michael, *International Law and the Arctic* (Cambridge University Press, Cambridge: 2013).

Caminos, Hugo, 'Categories of International Straits Excluded from the Transit Passage Regime under Part III of the United Nations Convention on the Law of the Sea,' in Tafsir Malick Ndiaye and Rűdiger Wolfrum (eds) *Law of the Sea, Environautical milesental Law and Settlement of Disputes* (Martinus Nijhoff, Leiden: 2007) 583–592.

Charney, Jonathan I. and Lewis M. Alexander (eds), *International Maritime Boundaries* Vol I (Martinus Nijhoff, Dordrecht/Boston: 1993).

Chircop, Aldo, 'Jurisdiction over ice-covered areas and the Polar Code: an emerging symbiotic relationship' (2016) 22 *Journal of International Maritime Law* 275–290.

Chircop, Aldo, 'The Growth of International Shipping in the Arctic: Is a Regulatory Review Timely?' (2009) 24 *International Journal of Marine and Coastal Law* 355–380.

Chircop, Aldo, 'The IMO, Its Role under UNCLOS and Its Polar Shipping Regulation' in Robert C. Beckman et al (eds), *Governance of Arctic Shipping: Balancing Rights and Interests of Arctic States and User States* (Brill/Nijhoff: Leiden/Boston: 2017) 107–143.

Coates, K.S. et al, *Arctic Front: Defending Canada in the Far North* (Thomas Allen, Toronto: 2008).

Cohen, Maxwell, 'The Arctic and the National Interest' (1970) 26 *International Journal* 52.

Conley, Heather A. et al, *The New Foreign Policy Frontier: U.S. Interests and Actors in the Arctic* (Centre for Strategic & International Studies, Washington: 2013).

Cooper, Helene, 'In a First, Chinese Navy Sails Off Alaska' *The New York Times* (2 September 2015), at: http://www.nytimes.com/2015/09/03/world/asia/in-a-first-chinese-navy-sails-off-alaska.html (last accessed on 1 November 2017).

Coppes, Mieke and Victoria Herrmann, *First Past the Pole: Harper, Trudeau, and Canada's Arctic Values* (The Arctic Institute, Centre for Circumpolar Security Studies, Washington: October 30, 2015) at http://www.thearcticinstitute.org/2015/10/first-past-the-pole.html (last accessed on 1 November 2017).

Crawford, James, *Brownlie's Principles of Public International Law* 8th (Clarendon Press, Oxford: 2012).

Critchley, W. Harriet, 'Polar Deployment of Soviet Submarines' (1984) 39 *International Journal* 828–865.

Cuyvers, Luc, *The Strait of Dover* (Martinus Nijhoff, Dordrecht: 1986).

de La Fayette, Louise A., 'Oceans Governance in the Arctic' (2008) 23 *International Journal of Marine and Coastal Law* 531–566.

de Mestral, Armand, 'Article 234 of the United Nations Convention on the Law of the Sea: Its Origins and Future' in Suzanne Lalonde and Ted L McDorman (eds), *International Law and the Politics of the Arctic Ocean: Essays in Honour of Donat Pharand* (Brill, Leiden/Boston: 2015) 111–124.

Department of Defense (USA), *Report to Congress on Arctic Operations and the Northwest Passage* (Department of Defense, Washington: May 2011).

Emmerson, Charles, *The Future History of the Arctic* (Public Affairs, London: 2010).

Faringdon, Hugh, *Strategic Geography: NATO, the Warsaw Pact, and the Superpowers* 2nd (Routledge, London: 1989).

Franckx, Erik and Laura Boone, 'Section 8 Ice-covered areas Article 234 Ice-covered areas' in Alexander Proelss (ed), *United Nations Convention on the Law of the Sea: A Commentary* (C.H.Beck/Hart/Nomos, Müchen/Oxford/Baden-Baden: 2017) 1566.

Franckx, Erik, *Maritime Claims in the Arctic: Canadian and Russian Perspectives* (Martinus Nijhoff, Dordrecht/Boston/London: 1993).

Friedman, Lisa, 'Trump Administration Moves to Open Arctic Refuge to Drilling Studies' *The New York Times* (September 16, 2017) at: https://www.nytimes.com/2017/09/16/climate/trump-arctic-refuge-drilling.html (last accessed on 1 November 2017).

Government of Canada, 'Canada's Northern Strategy' at: http://www.canadainternational.gc.ca/eu-ue/policies-politiques/arctic-arctique.aspx?lang=eng (last accessed on 1 November 2017).

Government of Canada, 'Statement on Canada's Arctic Foreign Policy' (2013) at: http://www.international.gc.ca/arctic-arctique/assets/pdfs/canada_arctic_foreign_policy-eng.pdf (last accessed on 1 November 2017).

Government of the United States of America, 'Executive Order: Enhancing Coordination of National Efforts in the Arctic' (21 January 2015), at: https://obamawhitehouse.archives.gov/the-press-office/2015/01/21/executive-order-enhancing-coordination-national-efforts-arctic (last accessed on 1 November 2017).

Grant, Shelagh D., *Polar Imperative: A History of Arctic Sovereignty in North America* (Douglas & McIntyre, Vancouver: 2010).

Gunnarsson, Bjorn, 'The Future of Arctic Marine Operations and Shipping Logistics' in Oran R. Young, Jong Deog Kim and Yoon Hyung Kim (eds), *The Arctic in World Affairs* (Korea Maritime Institute/East-West Centre, Seoul/Honolulu: 2013) 37–61.

Guschin, Arthur, 'China, Iceland and the Arctic' *The Diplomat* (May 20, 2015) at: https://thediplomat.com/2015/05/china-iceland-and-the-arctic/ (last accessed on 1 November 2017).

Han, Deukhoon (Peter) and Sung-Woo Lee, 'Rights, Interests, Positions and Practices of Asian Flag States, with Special Reference to the Republic of Korea' in Robert C. Beckman et al (eds), *Governance of Arctic Shipping: Balancing Rights and Interests of Arctic States and User States* (Brill/Nijhoff: Leiden/Boston: 2017) 299–317.

Harper, Stephen, 'Prime Minister Stephen Harper announces new Arctic Offshore Patrol Ships' (9 July 2007) at: https://www.canada.ca/en/news/archive/2007/07/prime-minister-stephen-harper-announces-new-arctic-offshore-patrol-ships.html (last accessed on 1 November 2017).

Hartsig, Andrew et al, 'Arctic Bottleneck: Protecting the Bering Strait from Increased Vessel Traffic', (2012) 10 *Ocean and Coastal Law Journal* 35–87.

Headland, R.K., 'Ten decades of transits of the Northwest Passage' (2010) 33 *Polar Geography* 1–2.

Henriksen, Tore, 'Norway, Denmark (in respect of Greenland) and Iceland' in Robert C. Beckman et al (eds), *Governance of Arctic Shipping* (Brill/Nijhoff, Leiden/Boston: 2017) 245.

Hertell, Hans H., 'Arctic melt: the tipping point for an Arctic Treaty' (2009) 21 *Georgetown International Environmental Law Review* 565–589.

Hirschfeld Davis, Julie, 'Obama, Visiting Arctic, Will Pledge Aid to Alaskans Hit by Climate Change' *The New York Times* (2 September 2015) at: http://www.nytimes.com/2015/09/03/us/politics/obama-arctic-alaska-climate-change.html?_r=0 (last accessed on 1 November 2017).

Ho, Joshua H., 'The Arctic Meltdown and Its Implications for Ports and Shipping in Asia' in James Kraska (ed), *Arctic Security in an Age of Climate Change* (Cambridge University Press, Cambridge: 2011) 33–43.

Honderich, John, *Arctic Imperative: Is Canada Losing the North?* (University of Toronto Press, Toronto: 1987).

Huebert, Rob, 'Article 234 and Marine Pollution Jurisdiction in the Arctic', in Oude Elferink, Alex G and Rothwell, Donald R. (eds), *The Law of the Sea and Polar Maritime Delimitation and Jurisdiction* (The Hague: Martinus Nijhoff, The Hague: 2001) 249–267.

Jabour, Julia and Melissa Weber, 'Is it Time to Cut the Gordian Knot of Polar Sovereignty?' (2008) 17 *Review of European Community and International Environmental Law* 27–40.

Jakes, Lara, 'Critics lukewarm on plans in Arctic' *Battleboro Reformer* (May 13, 2013) at: http://www.reformer.com/stories/critics-lukewarm-on-plans-in-arctic,382452 (last accessed on 1 November 2017).

Jares, Vladimir, 'The Continental Shelf Beyond 200 Nautical Miles: The Work of the Commission on the Limits of the Continental Shelf and the Arctic' (2009) 42 *Vanderbilt Journal of Transnational Law* 1265–1306.

Jennings, R. and A. Watts (1992), *Oppenheim's International Law*, 9th, vol I: Pts 2–4, (Longman: Harlow, UK).

Jensen, Leif Christian and Geir Hønneland (eds), *Handbook of the Politics of the Arctic* (Edward Elgar, Cheltenham, UK: 2015).

Jessup, Phillip C. and Howard J Taubenfeld, *Controls for Outer Space and the Antarctic Analogy*, (Columbia University Press, New York: 1959).

Jia, Bing Bing, 'Article 39 Duties of ships and aircraft during transit passage' in Alexander Proelss (ed), *United Nations Convention on the Law of the Sea: A Commentary* (C.H.Beck/Hart/Nomos, Müchen/Oxford/Baden-Baden, 2017) 300–305.

Joling, Dan, 'US Coast Guard studies shipping lanes for Bering Sea routes' *Alaska Dispatch News* (17 November 2015), at: https://www.adn.com/arctic/article/coast-guard-studies-shipping-lanes-bering-sea-routes/2015/11/17/ (last accessed on 1 November 2017).

Kaye, Stuart B., *The Torres Strait* (Martinus Nijhoff, Boston: 1997).

Klein, Natalie, *Maritime Security and the Law of the Sea* (Oxford University Press, Oxford: 2011).

Koivurova, Timo and VanderZwaag, David L., 'The Arctic Council at 10 years: retrospect and prospects' (2007) 40 *University of British Columbia Law Review* 121–194.

Koivurova, Timo, 'Environmental protection in the Arctic and Antarctic: can the polar regimes learn from each other?' (2005) 33 *International Journal of Legal Information* 204–281.

Koivurova, Timo, 'Limits and possibilities of the Arctic Council in a rapidly changing scene of Arctic governance'" (2010) 46 (237) *Polar Record* 146.

Koivurova, Timo, 'The Actions of Arctic States Respecting the Continental Shelf: A Reflective Essay' (2011) 42 *Ocean Development and International Law* 211–226.

Kramer, Andrew E., 'Polar thaw opens shortcut for Russian gas; New shipping lanes ease access to Chinese market for energy companies' (9 July 2013) *International Herald Tribune* 14.

Kraska, James (ed), *Arctic Security in a Age of Climate Change* (Cambridge University Press, Cambridge: 2011).

Kraska, James, 'Governance of Ice-Covered Areas: Rule Construction in the Arctic Ocean' (2014) 45 *Ocean Development and International Law* 260–271.

Kraska, James, 'The Northern Canada Vessel Traffic Services Zone Regulations (NORDREG) and the Law of the Sea' (2015) 30 *International Journal of Marine and Coastal Law* 225–254.

Lackenbauer, P. Whitney and James Manicom, 'Asian states and the Arctic: national perspectives on regional governance' in Leif Christian Jensen and Geir Hønneland (eds), *Handbook of the Politics of the Arctic* (Edward Elgar, Cheltenham (UK): 2015) 517.

Leifer, Michael, *International Straits of the World: Malacca, Singapore and Indonesia* (Sijthoff & Noordhoff, Alphen Aan Den Rijn: 1978).

Macnab, Ron, '"Use it or lose it" in Arctic Canada: action agenda or election hype?' (2009) 34 *Vermont Law Review* 3–14.

McDorman, Ted L., 'In the Wake of the Polar Sea: Canadian Jurisdiction and the Northwest Passage', (1986) 10 *Marine Policy* 243–257.

McDorman, Ted L., *Salt Water Neighbors: International Ocean Law Relations between the United States and Canada* (Oxford University Press, New York: 2009).

McRae, D.M. and D.J. Goundrey, 'Environmental Jurisdiction in the Arctic Waters: The Extent of Article 234', (1982) 16 *University of British Colombia Law Review* 197–228.

Mendez, Tessa, 'Thin Ice, Shifting Geopolitics: The Legal Implications of Arctic Ice Melt' (2009–2010) 38 *Denver Journal of International Law and Policy* 527–547.

Milman, Oliver, David Smith and Damian Carrington, 'Donald Trump confirms US will quit Paris climate agreement' *The Guardian* (2 June 2017) at: https://www.theguardian.com/environauticalmilesent/2017/jun/01/donald-trump-confirms-us-will-quit-paris-climate-deal (last accessed on 1 November 2017).

Molenaar, E.J., 'Arctic Marine Shipping: Overview of the International Legal Framework, Gaps, and Options' (2009) 18 *Journal of Transnational Law and Policy* 289–325.

Molenaar, Erik J., 'The Arctic, the Arctic Council, and the Law of the Sea' in Robert C. Beckman et al (eds), *Governance of Arctic Shipping: Balancing Rights and Interests of Arctic States and User States* (Brill/Nijhoff: Leiden/Boston: 2017) 24.

Molenaar, Erik Jaap, *Coastal State Jurisdiction over Vessel-Source Pollution* (Kluwer Law International, The Hague: 1998).

Morris, Michael A., *The Strait of Magellan* (Martinus Nijhoff, Dordrecht: 1989).

Nandan, Satya N. and Shabtai Rosenne, *United Nations Convention on the Law of the Sea 1982: A Commentary* Vol II (Martinus Nijhoff, Dordrecht: 1993).

Nash, Marian, *Cumulative Digest of United States Practice in International Law 1981–1988* Book II (Department of State, Washington: 1994).

Nihan, Ünlü, *The legal regime of the Turkish Straits* (Martinus Nijhoff, The Hague: 2002).

Nilsen, Thomas, 'Murmansk and Arkhangelsk population continues to decline' *The Independent Barents Observer* (September 28, 2017) at: https://thebarentsobserver.com/en/life-and-public/2017/09/murmansk-and-arkhangelsk-population-continues-decline (last accessed on 1 November 2017).

Ostreng, Willy, 'The Northern Sea Route: a new era in Soviet policy?' (1991) 22 *Ocean Development and International Law* 259–287.

Oude Elferink, Alex G., 'Maritime Delimitation Between Denmark/Greenland and Norway' (2007) 38 *Ocean Development and International Law* 375–380.

Oude Elferink, Alex G., 'The Arctic Sunrise incident: a multi-faceted law of the sea case with a human rights dimension' (2014) 29 *International Journal of Marine and Coastal Law* 244–289.

Pharand, Donat, 'Canada's Sovereignty over the Northwest Passage' (1989) 10 *Michigan Journal of International Law* 653.

Pharand, Donat, 'Sovereignty in the Arctic: The International Legal Context' in Edgar J. Dosman (ed), *Sovereignty and Security in the Arctic* (London: Routledge, London: 1989) 145.

Pharand, Donat, 'The Arctic Waters and the Northwest Passage: A Final Revisit' (2007) 38 *Ocean Development and International Law* 3.

Pharand, Donat, 'The Northwest Passage in International Law' (1979) 17 *Canadian Yearbook of International Law* 99.

Pharand, Donat, *Canada's Arctic Waters in International Law* (Cambridge University Press, Cambridge: 1988).

Pharand, Donat, *The Law of the Sea of the Arctic with Special Reference to Canada* (University of Ottawa Press, Ottawa: 1973).

Pharand, Donat, *The Northwest Passage Arctic Straits* (Martinus Nijhoff, Dordrecht: 1984).

Powell, Richard C. and Klaus Dodds (eds), *Polar Geopolitics?* (Edward Elgar, Cheltenham, UK: 2014).

President of the United States, *National Strategy for the Arctic Region* (White House, Washington: 2013).

Pullen, T.C., 'What Price Canadian Sovereignty?' (1987) 113 (9) *Proceedings of the US Naval Institute* 66.

Purver, R., 'Security and arms control at the poles' (1984) XXXIX *International Journal* 888.

Richter-Menge, J., J.E. Overland, J. Mathis, 'Arctic Report Card: Update for 2016' (December 6, 2016) at: http://www.arctic.noaa.gov/Report-Card/Report-Card-2016/ArtMID/5022/ArticleID/270/Executive-Summary (last accessed on 1 November 2017).

Roach, Ashley and Smith, Robert W., *Excessive Maritime Claims* 3rd (Martinus Nijhoff, Leiden: 2012).

Roach, J. Ashley, 'The Polar Code and Its Adequacy' in Robert C. Beckman et al (eds), *Governance of Arctic Shipping* (Brill/Nijhoff, Leiden/Boston: 2017) 144.

Roach, John, 'Arctic Ice at All-Time Low' National Geographic News, August 20, 2007, at: https://news.nationalgeographic.com/news/2007/08/070820–global-warming.html (last accessed on 1 November 2017).

Roach, John, "Arctic Melt Opens Northwest Passage," National Geographic News, September 17, 2007, at: http://news.nationalgeographoc.com/news/pf/38614724.html (last accessed on 1 November 2017).

Rothwell, Donald R., 'International Straits and UNCLOS: An Australian Case Study' (1992) 23 *Journal of Maritime Law and Commerce* 461–483.

Rothwell, Donald R. and Stephens, Tim, *The International Law of the Sea* 2nd (Hart, Oxford: 2016).

Rothwell, Donald R., 'Arctic sovereignty and its legal significance for Canada' in Leif Christian Jensen and Geir Hønneland (eds), *Handbook of the Politics of the Arctic* (Edward Elgar, Cheltenham (UK): 2015) 247–261.

Rothwell, Donald R., 'Canada and the United States' in Robert C. Beckman et al (eds), *Governance of Arctic Shipping: Balancing Rights and Interests of Arctic States and User States* (Brill/Nijhoff: Leiden/Boston: 2017) 217.

Rothwell, Donald R., 'Polar Oceans Governance in the Twenty-First Century' (2012) 26 *Ocean Yearbook* 343–360.

Rothwell, Donald R., 'Polar opposites: environmental discourses and management in Antarctica and the Arctic' in Brad Jessup and Kim Rubenstein (eds), *Environmental Discourses in Public and International Law* (Cambridge University Press, Cambridge: 2012) 355–374.

Rothwell, Donald R., 'The Arctic in International Affairs: Time for a New Regime?' (2008) XV (1) *Brown Journal of World Affairs* 241–253.

Rothwell, Donald R., 'The Canadian – U.S. Northwest Passage Dispute: A Reassessment' (1993) 26 *Cornell International Law Journal* 331–372.

Rothwell, Donald R., *The Polar Regions and the Development of International Law* (Cambridge University Press, Cambridge: 1996).

Rothwell, Donald R., 'The Arctic Environmental Protection Strategy and International Environmental Cooperation in the Far North' (1995) 6 *Yearbook of International Environmental Law* 65–105.

Sevunts, Levon, 'Census 2016: Nunavut leads Canada's population growth' *Eye on the Arctic* (8 February 2017) at: http://www.rcinet.ca/eye-on-the-arctic/2017/02/08/census-2016–nunavut-leads-canadas-population-growth/ (last accessed on 1 November 2017).

Shaw, M.N., *International Law* 6th (Cambridge: Cambridge University Press, Cambridge: 2008).

Smedal, G., *Acquisition of Sovereignty over Polar Areas* (I Kommisjon Hos Jacob Dybwad, Oslo: 1931).

Solski, Jan, 'Russia' in Robert C. Beckman et al (eds), *Governance of Arctic Shipping* (Brill/Nijhoff, Leiden/Boston: 2017) 173–216.

Staalesen, Atle, 'China is building its second icebreaker domestically' *Arctic Now* (28 September 2017) at: https://www.arcticnow.com/business/shipping/2017/09/28/china-is-building-its-second-icebreaker-domestically/ (last accessed on 1 November 2017).

Staalesen, Atle, 'Terrorism is coming to the Arctic, Putin fears' *The Independent Barents Observer* (December 29, 2015) at: https://thebarentsobserver.com/en/security/2015/12/terrorism-coming-arctic-putin-fears (last accessed on 1 November 2017).

Stephens, Tim, 'The Arctic and Antarctic Regimes and the Limits of Polar Comparativism' (2011) 54 *German Yearbook of International Law* 315–349.

Stevenson, C., 'Hans off! The struggle for Hans Island and the potential ramifications for international border dispute resolution' (2007) 30 *Boston College International and Comparative Law Review* 263–275.

Svarlien, O., 'The Sector Principle in Law and Practice', (1960) 10 *Polar Record* 248–63.

Thomas, A.R. and James C. Duncan (eds), 'Annotated Supplement to The Commanders Handbook on the Law of Naval Operations' (1999) 73 *International Legal Studies* 205.

Timchenko, Leonid, 'The Northern Sea Route: Russian Management and Jurisdiction over Navigation in Arctic Seas', in Alex G. Oude Elferink and Donald R. Rothwell (eds), *The Law of the Sea and Polar Maritime Delimitation and Jurisdiction* (Martinus Nijhoff, The Hague: 2001) 269–291.

Titley, David W. and Courtney C. St. John, 'Arctic Security Considerations and the U.S. Navy's "Arctic Roadmap"' in James Kraska (ed), *Arctic Security in an Age of Climate Change* (Cambridge University Press, Cambridge: 2011) 267–280.

Triggs, Gillian D., *International Law and Australian Sovereignty in Antarctica* (Legal Books, Sydney: 1986).

Truver, Scott C., *The Strait of Gibraltar and the Mediterranean* (Sijthoff & Noordhoff, Alphen Aan Den Rijn: 1980).

United States Coast Guard, *Arctic Strategy* (United States Coast Guard, Washington: 2013).

United States of America, 'Arctic Region Policy' National Security Presidential Directive/NSPD – 66; Homeland Security Presidential Directive/HSPD – 25, 9 January 2009.

Valencia, Mark J. and Abu Bakar Jaafar, 'Environautical milesental Management of the Malacca – Singapore Straits: legal and institutional issues' (1985) 25 *Natural Resources Journal* 195–232.

Vidas, Davor (ed), *Protecting the Polar Marine Environment: Law and Policy for Pollution Prevention* (Cambridge University Press, Cambridge: 2000).

Wadhams, Peter, *A Farewell to Ice* (Allen Lane, London: 2016).

Walker, George K., 'Definitions for the 1982 Law of the Sea Convention – Part II: Analysis of the IHO Consolidated Glossary' (2003) 33 *California Western International Law Journal* 219.

Watson, Molly, 'An Arctic treaty: a solution to the international dispute over the polar region' (2009) 14 *Ocean and Coastal Law Journal* 307–334.

Weber, Bob, 'Canada, Denmark should turn Hans Island into a condominium: academics' *CBC News* (November 12, 2015) at: http://www.cbc.ca/news/canada/north/canada-denautical milesark-should-turn-hans-island-into-a-condominium-academics-1.3315640 (last accessed on 1 November 2017).

Weber, Mel, 'Defining the outer limits of the continental shelf across the Arctic basin: the Russian submission, states' rights, boundary delimitation and Arctic regional cooperation' (2009) 24 *International Journal of Marine and Coastal Law* 653–681.

Young, Oran R., Jong Deog Kim and Yoon Hyung Kim (eds), *The Arctic in World Affairs* (Korea Maritime Institute/East-West Centre, Seoul/Honolulu: 2013).

Yuan woon, Chih, 'China, Canada and framings of Arctic geopolitics' in Richard C. Powell and Klaus Dodds (eds), *Polar Geopolitics*? (Edward Elgary, Cheltenham (UK): 2014) 166–182.

Zellen, Barry Scott, 'Where East and West converge: the US embrace of collaborative security for the Arctic' in Leif Christian Jensen and Geir Hønneland (eds), *Handbook of the Politics of the Arctic* (Edward Elgar, Cheltenham (UK): 2015) 550–572.

Zysk, Katarzyna, 'Military Aspects of Russia's Arctic Policy: Hard Power and Natural Resources' in James Kraska (ed), *Arctic Security in an Age of Climate Change* (Cambridge University Press, Cambridge: 2011) 85–106.

www.ingramcontent.com/pod-product-compliance
Lightning Source LLC
Chambersburg PA
CBHW071355230926
51846CB00002B/570
* 9 7 8 9 0 0 4 3 6 3 8 7 8 *